A critical and bibliographical series

General Editor
Ian Scott-Kilvert

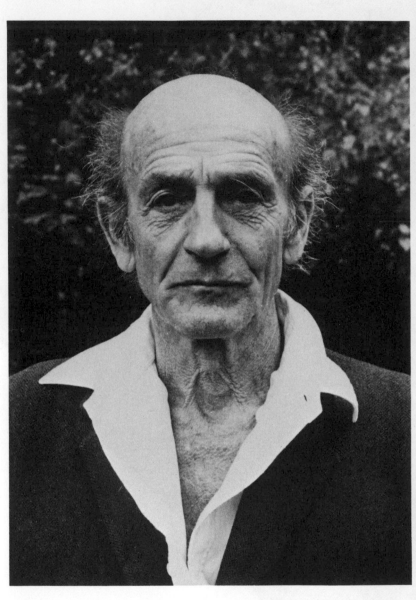

F. R. LEAVIS

F. R. LEAVIS

by

EDWARD GREENWOOD

PUBLISHED FOR
THE BRITISH COUNCIL
BY LONGMAN GROUP LTD

LONGMAN GROUP LTD
Longman House, Burnt Mill, Harlow, Essex

Associated companies, branches and
representatives throughout the world

First published 1978
© Edward Greenwood 1978

Printed in England by
Bradleys, Reading and London

ISBN 0 582 01274 0

CONTENTS

¶ F. R. LEAVIS was born in Cambridge on 14 July 1895 and died on 14 April 1978.

F. R. LEAVIS

I. LIFE

FRANK RAYMOND LEAVIS was born in Cambridge on 14 July 1895, and educated at the Perse School and Emmanuel College, Cambridge. He served in the First World War in an ambulance unit as a stretcher bearer carrying, it is said, a pocket Milton all through the ordeal. It was no doubt his having lived through those times which made it impossible for him to endorse the sublime simplicity of Trotsky's reference to the '2nd of August, 1914, when the maddened power of bourgeois culture let loose upon the world the blood and fire of an imperialistic war'. In his essay 'T. S. Eliot as Critic' in *Anna Karenina and Other Essays* Leavis speaks of 'those early years after the great hiatus', when he 'struggled to achieve the beginnings of articulate thought about literature'. He first read History and then English as an undergraduate, becoming a student in the newly founded English School for the second part of the Tripos. The figures who 'really counted' in the achieving of his 'articulate thought about literature' were George Santayana (despite this 'not fundamentally congenial') and Matthew Arnold. To them was added Eliot's own influence as a critic. Leavis bought *The Sacred Wood* in 1920. Along with these went the influence of the writing in Ford Madox Ford's (or Hueffer's) *The English Review*, to which Leavis had subscribed as a schoolboy back in 1912 and in which he had made his first acquaintance with D. H. Lawrence's writing ('The Prussian Officer'). Leavis was impressed by Ford's acceptance of the view that in the 'irreversible new conditions' of modern industrial civilization the concern for 'the higher cultural values' must be restricted to a small minority, while at the same time that concern must concede nothing 'to the preciousness, fatuity or spirit of Aestheticism'. That same view was to be a cornerstone of the enterprise of Leavis's own periodical *Scrutiny*. It was this which made Leavis outraged when Brother George Every suggested in his *Poetry and Personal Responsibility* that 'The error of the *Scrutiny* writers was to look for the intelligentsia in the same place where aesthetes were recruited in the days of the Yellow Book and the Rhymers' Club.'

Leavis was stimulated by such teachers in the new English School as Mansfield D. Forbes and I. A. Richards, who will be discussed at greater length in the second section of this essay. He wrote a doctoral thesis on the periodical literature of the eighteenth century with particular reference to Addison's *The Spectator*, and this further contributed to his lifelong concern with the way in which the ethos of a periodical can both reflect and mould the cultural aspirations of a wider public. His wife was, of course, to carry on this interest in the social relations between literature and its public in her classic study (which grew out of a doctoral thesis) *Fiction and the Reading Public* (1932).

Leavis also greatly admired the periodical *The Calendar of Modern Letters* edited by Edgell Rickword. It ran from 1925 to mid 1927, and though retrospectively Leavis was to see its failure 'to win the interest and loyalty of a sufficient public to keep it alive' as an index of cultural decline, its concern with the maintenance of critical standards was to be an important inspiration of his own editing. *The Calendar of Modern Letters* ran a series of intelligent deflations of what it saw as the exaggerated reputations of such contemporary figures as H. G. Wells, J. M. Barrie, G. K. Chesterton and John Galsworthy (the Galsworthy critique was written by D. H. Lawrence): these articles were later collected by Edgell Rickword under the title *Scrutinies*. Leavis was to call the periodical he founded in 1932 *Scrutiny*, and in the following year he published a selection of material from *The Calendar* with an appreciative preface under the title *Towards Standards of Criticism*.

By 1925 Leavis was doing some supervision teaching of English literature at Emmanuel. D. W. Harding, who was later to be a fellow editor of *Scrutiny*, recalled his dynamism as a teacher when, looking back fifty years in a broadcast symposium in 1975, he said:

He was really superb. I remember the feelings with which this other man and I would come away. We would be partly exhilarated, and partly a bit subdued and rueful, perhaps. Exhilarated because of the new insights and the fine discriminations he had made, and sobered because he kept such extremely high standards in insight and one just realised how unskilled one was as a reader. At the same time, there was no feeling that he belittled you in any way—if you had difficulties or raised objections, then he met you on those. He could scrap what he was going to say and just meet you on whatever you were interested in.

In 1929 Leavis married Queenie Roth, and the next few years brought a wonderful harvest of critical work culminating in the *annus mirabilis* of 1932 when Leavis published *New Bearings in English Poetry*, his wife published *Fiction and the Reading Public* and the quarterly periodical *Scrutiny* was founded. In view of the not wholly unjustified accusation that *Scrutiny* in its later years was hostile to contemporary literature, it is worth stressing that the young Leavis was in the vanguard in this matter. He incurred the displeasure of the university authorities and the English Faculty by lecturing on *Ulysses* to his classes in the mid 1920s. He recalls 'conventional academics' saying of him at the time of Lawrence's death in 1930, 'We don't like the kind of book he lends undergraduates'. At this time the Faculty Librarian sanctioned the withholding of D. H. Lawrence's and T. F. Powys's works from undergraduates who wanted to borrow them or read them in the library. As to the teaching of contemporary work in the 1930s, Professor Muriel Bradbrook recalls Leavis's interest in the poetry of I. A. Richards's pupil, the ex-student of mathematics William Empson. She says: 'It cannot be very often that undergraduates are taught the poetry of a fellow undergraduate, but we were taught about some of Empson's poems by Leavis.'

Leavis had enemies in the English Faculty, however, and all this brilliance and the *Scrutiny* project did not enable him to obtain, as in all justice it should have, a permanent Faculty post. At last in 1936 (the year in which *Revaluation* appeared) he was made a Lecturer at the age of forty-one, after having been a Probationary (or Assistant) Lecturer since 1927, and after having seen a younger candidate given precedence over him. All this was to be a source of great bitterness to him both at the time and in later years. Leavis had moved from Emmanuel to Downing in 1929 and was elected a Fellow there in 1936 after the Faculty had made him a Lecturer. *Revaluation*, which contained material from *Scrutiny* articles, yet has unity as a book in mapping out a new history of English poetry, as Professor René Wellek recognized at the time when he wrote: 'It seems the first consistent attempt to rewrite the history of English poetry from the twentieth-century point of view'. It is not annalistic but critical history, history concerned with making first-hand judgments distinguishing the first-rate from the second-rate. It does not make the mistake of F. W. Bateson in his *English Poetry and the English Language* (1935), which was to suppose that critical judgment can find its validation in a combination of assertions about social and linguistic history. In reviewing F. W. Bateson's book Leavis found Bateson's view of language involved excessive reliance on a too simple 'denotation'/'connotation' dichotomy and a too naïve view of the nature of critical judgment. The two critics were to clash again on the subject of literary history when F. W. Bateson attacked Leavis's reading of Marvell's poem 'A Dialogue between the Soul and Body' in an article in *Essays in Criticism* in January 1953. Leavis pointed out that the historical context in which Bateson proposed to anchor the reading of the poem was something much less determinate than the poem itself, to whose complexities his reading was manifestly inadequate: 'the most essential kind of knowledge can come only from an intelligent frequentation of the poetry'.

The Great Tradition, published in 1948, did for the English novel what *Revaluation* had done for English poetry: it provided us with literary history that possessed an essential focus or centre of interest. *The Common Pursuit* (1952) collected many of Leavis's best articles from *Scrutiny*. *D. H. Lawrence: Novelist* (1955) showed a falling off for those who could not see Lawrence as so flawless a writer as Leavis does, and has a significantly greater amount of pure quotation and of exclamatory praise as opposed to the close analytic criticism which is Leavis's distinction. There was then a twelve-year gap in books before *Anna Karenina and Other Essays* (1967) inaugurated a rich spate of works (some, notably *Dickens the Novelist* (1970), joint productions with his wife) written during Leavis's seventies. The Dickens book, the engagement with Lawrence's text in *Thought, Words and Creativity* (1976) and with Eliot's *Four Quartets* in *The Living Principle* (1975) showed a welcome return to Leavis's true strength, the discussion of particular examples of prose and poetry, after the in some ways less satisfactory engagement with more general matters of wider cultural health in such works as *English Literature in our Time and the University* (1969) and, in particular, *Nor Shall My Sword* (1972). The latter contains Leavis's attack of 1962 on C. P. Snow which introduces the interesting idea of the 'third realm' as a name for the mode of existence of works of literature. They are not merely private, like a dream, nor public in the sense of something that can be tripped over, but exist only in human minds as a work of collaborative re-constitution. Much in the lecture and the book, however, is too personal in the wrong sense of the word and lacks the fuller disinterestedness of Leavis at his best. If humanity has the creativeness which Leavis attributes to it, there is no need, perhaps, to strike such a note of despair at the state of institutions such as the University.

Leavis was appointed Reader in English at Cambridge in 1960 and held this post until his retirement from the Faculty in 1962. He was appointed Visiting Professor of English at the University of York from 1965–68 and subsequently held Visiting Professorships at the Universities of Wales and of Bristol. He was awarded Doctorates of Literature by the Universities of Leeds, York, Queen's Belfast, Delhi and Aberdeen. He was made a Companion of Honour in the New Year's list for 1978. He died on 14 April 1978 at the age of eighty-two.

II. THE SIGNIFICANCE OF LEAVIS'S CRITICISM

To try to bring out what is special about Leavis's approach to literary criticism I will begin by quoting a page from the preface of *Towards Standards in Criticism*:

Literary criticism provides the test for life and concreteness; where it degenerates, the instruments of thought degenerate too, and thinking, released from the testing and energizing contact with the full living consciousness, is debilitated, and betrayed to the academic, the abstract and the verbal.

Behind this lies a famous passage in Pound's *How to Read* which Leavis quoted and endorsed in his own 'How To Teach Reading' (1932), later reprinted as an appendix to *Education and the University* (1943). Pound wrote that literature

has to do with the clarity of 'any and every' thought and opinion. It has to do with maintaining the very cleanliness of the tools, the health of the very matter of thought itself. Save the rare and very limited instances of invention in the plastic arts, or in mathematics, the individual cannot think or communicate his thought, the governor and legislator cannot act effectively or frame his laws, without words, and the solidity and validity of these words is in the care of the damned and despised *literati*. When their work goes rotten—by that I do not mean when they express indecorous thoughts—but when their very medium, the very essence of their work, the application of word to thing goes rotten, i.e. becomes slushy and inexact, or excessive or bloated, the whole machinery of social and of individual thought and order goes to pot.

The view as to the intimate relation between the health of language and the health of consciousness which underlines both passages has, of course, been held by figures as diverse as Ruskin, Arnold, Collingwood, Wittgenstein, Kenneth Burke and George Orwell. But there is one especially important point which a close reading of the Leavis passage can bring out. That is the answer to the question which puzzles many who have only a peripheral acquaintance with Leavis's work as the work of one among many writers on literature, the Lewises, Tillyards, Fryes, Trillings, Kermodes and Blooms—namely 'what is all this fuss about one teacher of English, and one in an English provincial backwater at that?' Leaving aside the question as to whether Cambridge was a provincial backwater (though I think many would still endorse Leavis's remark that 'The British university as represented by Oxford and Cambridge was a distinct and strongly positive organic life, rooted in history') the contention that 'literary criticism provides the test for life and concreteness' shows that 'literary criticism' has a meaning for Leavis quite different from that which it held for any of the writers on literature mentioned above. It becomes, in short, the central *organon* for humanistic studies.

There is an admirable definition of the poet's task by Hazlitt. He calls it that of 'unravelling the real web of associations, which have been woven round any subject by nature, and the unavoidable conditions of humanity'. But the poet is moved by such associations to picture such webs rather than to unravel them. The unravelling or 'explication' of such wholes, the refining and articulation of first-hand perceptions of them into delicate and relevant commentary is surely the task of the critic, and one which, incidentally, should obviate the standard and misleading move of fobbing him off as a failed creator or as a parasite on other men's works. No doubt Aristotle with his habitual common sense, remarked: 'It is a thing very difficult, if not impossible, for a man to be a good judge of what he himself cannot do'; but Aristotle, it should be remembered, divided doing or *praxis* into two parts, making things and performing actions. The passage just quoted from the *Politics*, 1340b, was on judging *musical* performance. But as regards made things, whether shoes or poems, Aristotle, like Plato, thought the 'user' not the maker was the best judge. When F. W. Bateson suggests in *Essays in Critical Dissent* that it would be a good thing for critics to give 'public evidence of their creative metal' by publishing examples of their poetic efforts, and remarks in his grudging survey of Leavis's work in *The Sewanee Review* (1977), on 'the curious absence in the typical *Scrutiny* critic of creative talent', his assumption has a gratuitous irrelevance about it. The notion that a critic must compose a poem as a sort of implicit guarantee that he can be trusted to talk about poetry is little short of grotesque. If we can't tell that from the discourse itself, no amount of sub-Tennysonian or sub-Audenesque 'poetastry' will help us.

It is certainly true that Leavis is an exception to the rule that all the major critics from Dryden to Eliot have written criticism as a counterpart to their creative efforts. In Dryden and Eliot in particular there is a constant atmosphere of the workshop. Johnson's criticism reflects (as Leavis's essays on him well bring out) both the strength and limitations of Augustan assumptions. Wordsworth's criticism is an apology for his own work, and much of Coleridge's is a defence of those divagations into the abstractions of German philosophy he had come to love. Arnold's criticism conspicuously demands from poetry what he is regretfully aware he cannot himself give as a poet. But it could be claimed that this complete lack of any *parti pris* as a practitioner, this putting of his whole energy into an encounter with the text, into the full realization of what is before him, is the very thing which enables Leavis to attain that 'peculiar completeness of response' which he believes it is the critic's task to achieve and to develop into commentary.

If there is sometimes animus in Leavis (and the account of his career shows that he had some warrant for resentment against the Cambridge English Faculty), that animus is, as Christopher Ricks pointed out in the broadcast symposium in 1975, closely linked to an animation which is inseparable from the intensity of conviction with which he tries to communicate his insights. Leavis's prose style has often been criticised by those whose ideal of prose is a kind of compound of Pater, Logan Pearsall Smith and Lord David Cecil, but he developed a prose style partly related no doubt to his spoken idiom with pupils, partly adapted (Ricks suggests) from Henry James (whose own style imitates 'oral' patterns) in which qualification and nuance involve an increment rather than a loss of energy. Criticism was ideally, for Leavis, a collaborative dialogue, and much of his life's work as a critic actually took the form of oral as well as written communication, in lectures, supervisions and seminars. He ended the introduction to *Revaluation* with the words: 'The debt that I wish to acknowledge is to those with whom I have, during the past dozen years, discussed literature as a "teacher": if I have learnt anything about the methods of profitable discussion I have learnt it in collaboration with them.' At the same time he expresses on more than one occasion his dislike of the suggestion of 'authoritative telling' associated with teaching. In *English Literature in Our Time and the University* he writes:

The peculiar nature of the study of English worth pursuing at university level entails its being in the most essential regards, though a special study, not what 'specialist' suggests. A genuine teacher doesn't find himself holding back his subtlest insight and his most adventurous thought because they are not suitable for communication to first- or second-year men. He tests and develops in 'teaching' his perceptions, his understanding and his thought, and with good men may do so very fruitfully. For what we call teaching is, if genuine, a matter of enlisting and fostering collaboration; the teacher in English has, in what I have pointed to in the distinction between 'special' and 'specialist', a peculiar advantage—or a given kind of advantage in a peculiar form. The qualifications of a teacher are given in these observations. He is one who has the kinds of interest in literature that go with finding pleasure and profit in discussing it with intelligent young students.

Such discussion will of course have no truck with the notion of literature for literature's sake or the chimera of 'purely literary values'. There is no 'significant form' in literature providing an 'aesthetic emotion' to be exclaimed about in a way unrelated to one's other concerns and mode of life. Form in a work of literature can, for Leavis, 'only be a matter of significance such as can be intelligently and profitably discussed'. Literary values are bound up with moral and spiritual ones, and it is oddly enough this very fact which may lead to the puzzling phenomenon of 'the peculiar hatred any intelligent conception of the importance of English may expect to encounter in a university English School'. Leavis would entirely endorse his master Santayana's condemnation of any 'holding a single interest free from all others' as only making the aesthetic sphere contemptible in the end, and would agree with Santayana that 'Art being a part of life, the criticism of art is a part of morals'. In addition to this Leavis is strongly attracted to the view that it is good for those engaged in the political and social affairs of a nation to be affected by a climate touched by a vital literary culture.

I have spoken of Leavis's concern with putting his whole energy into an encounter with the text, and it would be as well to have a concrete example of his work in front of us before engaging further with the problems raised by his critical work as a whole. I therefore quote from pp. 108–110 of *The Living Principle* parts of the analysis of a speech from *The Revenger's Tragedy*. This has the advantage for purposes of economy that Leavis is analysing one passage not comparing two:

> Does the silkworm expend her yellow labours
> For thee? For thee does she undo herself?
> Are lordships sold to maintain ladyships
> For the poor benefit of a bewitching minute?
> Why does yon fellow falsify highways
> And lays his life between the judge's lips
> To refine such a one? Keeps horse and men
> To beat their valours for her?

The key word in the first line is 'expend'. In touch with 'spin', it acts with its force of 'spend' on the 'yellow', turning it to gold, and so, while adding directly to the suggestion of wealth and luxury, bringing out by a contrasting co-presence in the one word the soft yellowness of the silk. To refer to silk, emblem of luxurious leisure, as 'labours' is in itself a telescoping of conflicting associations. Here, then, in this slow, packed, self-pondering line (owing to the complex organization of meaning the reader finds he cannot skim easily over the words, or slip through them in a euphonious glide) we have the type of the complexity that gives the whole passage that rich effect of life and body. It relates closely to the theme of the play, but there is a vitality that is immediately apparent in the isolated extract, and we are concerned here with taking note of its obvious manifestations.

The nature of the imagery involved in

> lays his life between the judge's lips

might perhaps not be easy to define, but it is certainly an instance in which effectiveness is not mainly visual. The sense of being at the mercy of another's will and word is focused in a sensation of extreme physical precariousness, a sensation of lying helpless, on the point of being ejected at a breath into the abyss. In 'refine' we probably have another instance of a double meaning. In the first place 'refine' would mean 'make fine' or 'elegant' (the speaker is addressing the skull of his dead mistress). But the gold image, coming through by way of 'sold' (and the more effectively for never having been explicit), seems also to be felt here, with the

16

suggestion that nothing can refine this dross. In this way the structure of the last sentence is explained: horse and men are represented by their 'valours', their 'refined' worths, which are beaten for 'such a one', and so the contrast of the opening question is clinched—'her yellow labours for *thee*?'

III. THE PROBLEM SITUATION

In order to understand Leavis's work it is necessary to grasp the problem situation that faced him at the outset of his critical career and to touch further on the difficulties with the Cambridge English Faculty already mentioned. First of all we must remind ourselves how recent is the notion that the literature of the vernacular tongue could be made the centre of a humanistic education. Here the works of E. M. W. Tillyard *The Muse Unchained*, D. J. Palmer *The Rise of English Studies* and John Gross *The Rise and Fall of the Man of Letters* are all useful. When Matthew Arnold in the 1880s somewhat shakily defended the importance of literature in education as against T. H. Huxley's claims for the paramountcy of science, even Arnold only went so far as to say that the vernacular literature should be taught along with the classical literature of Greece and Rome. It was T. H. Huxley himself who suggested that the vernacular literature might stand alone as the vehicle of humanistic culture at a time when so many and varied educational demands were being made, though it must be confessed that Huxley's own emphasis on the 'how' of teaching fell forbiddingly on literature as philologically illustrative of the science of language, an idea which others were to build in to the Oxford English school when it was eventually founded.

It was perhaps the Cambridge philosopher Henry Sidgwick who first grasped philosophically the idea that the literature of the vernacular tongue could be made central to humanistic education. Because of this Mrs Q. D. Leavis was later to associate Sidgwick with his friend the critic and historian of ideas, Leslie Stephen, in a kind of Cambridge tradition to which she felt that the work of her husband, herself and their colleagues on the periodical *Scrutiny*, founded in May 1932,

17

could be linked: at the same time she wished to dissociate them from the other Cambridge tradition connected with the Bloomsbury of Stephen's daughter Virginia Woolf and her friend Desmond McCarthy (then the chief reviewer of *The Sunday Times* and an influential figure in literary journalism) and from the academicism of ex-classicists such as Tillyard. Mrs Leavis writes:

We believe with Stephen that criticism is not a mystic rapture but a process of the intelligence. No doubt the environment of Clerk Maxwell and Henry Sidgwick was peculiarly favourable to the development of such an attitude to literature, but we recollect that Arnold and Coleridge also practised this method when they were most effectual.

In 'Henry Sidgwick's Cambridge' which appeared in *Scrutiny* for 1947, and which includes a good brief account of Sidgwick's pioneering work for women's education, Mrs Leavis recurs to Sidgwick as wanting 'to pitch the Classics overboard' in favour of the study of English literature 'in association with other modern literatures', which is exactly F. R. Leavis's own programme in his *Education and the University*.

Despite such men as Sidgwick there was still considerable opposition to the founding of a chair of English literature and the inauguration of a Tripos examination in the subject at Cambridge. 'I wonder how many people realise that the first English Tripos examination was held as recently as 1919?' writes Basil Willey in the interesting, if reticent, account of Cambridge English from 1919 to 1964 in his *Cambridge and other Memories*. The philosopher McTaggart even said 'a Professorship of such a subject would not only be useless but positively harmful to the University'. Two men who soon came to the fore in the new school were Mansfield Forbes, a teacher of genius who wrote nothing, and the more widely known I. A. Richards. Leavis dedicated *English Literature in Our Time and the University* (1969) to the memory of Henry Chadwick (who had been instrumental in getting the study of English literature separated from the study of Old English—contrary to the state of things at Oxford) and of Forbes. Forbes himself emerges from the introduction to that book as a kind of proto-Leavis with something of Leavis's effect. Leavis writes:

Of course, he incidentally reinforced some conceits and exposed his influence to the charge of inspiring and equipping ambitious stupidities and stark insensibilities to posture as something else. But what 'teacher' can be insured against this kind of hazard? Where does safety lie unless in nullity? We didn't need Nietzsche to tell us to live dangerously; there is no other way of living. Forbes, himself a vital force of intelligence, had, in the strong disinterested way, the courage of life and, it follows, the impulse and the power to stir intelligence into active life in others.

When asked to comment on Edna St. Vincent Millay's sonnet 'What's this of death, from you who will never die?', Forbes's idiosyncratic vivacity produced the following:

This is a studied orgasm from a 'Shakespeare-R. Brooke' complex, as piece 7 from a 'Marvell-Wordsworth-Drinkwater, etc., stark-simplicity' complex. Hollow at first reading; resoundingly hollow at second. A sort of thermos vacuum, 'the very thing' for a digni-fied picnic in this sort of Two-Seater Sonnet. The 'Heroic' Hectoring of line I, the hearty quasi-stoical button-holing of the unimpeachably-equipped beloved, *the magisterial finger-wagging* of 'I tell you this'!! Via such conduits magnanimity may soon be laid on as an indispensable, if not obligatory, modern convenience.

These remarks were called out by a very famous experiment. I. A. Richards distributed unsigned and undated poems, a mixture of Shakespeare, Donne and other masters with pieces of inflated and sentimental trash and then collected and published selections from the 'protocol' reports on them by students and members of faculty in Part One of his book *Practical Criticism*. The significance of Richard's experiment for criticism has been well described by the best of the writers in *Scrutiny* after Leavis himself, D. W. Harding. Harding writes:

It is . . . possible to show that differences of opinion in literary matters frequently arise from errors of approach which even those who make them can be brought to recognize. With people who assert that they know what they like, the one hope is to demonstrate to them that in point of fact they *don't*, that according to standards they themselves recognize elsewhere, their judgment here is mistaken. As these inconsistencies are faced and abandoned, the possibility of agreement with other people grows greater.

Even if in the end we find irreducible differences of taste (and even then the procedure will have established *something*) Harding believes, as Leavis himself does, that much common territory can be discovered in this quasi-Socratic dialectical way before the stage of irreducible difference is reached. What are needed are not grandiose theories or rhapsodies about the adventures of one's soul among masterpieces or, for that matter, the dry purely external application of technical equipment from, say, linguistics, but 'fully illustrated discussions of actual instances'. These discussions will offer starting points for further investigations. They will 'draw attention to serious possibilities of misreading and misjudging' and will show that 'the adequate reading of poetry is a discipline and not a relaxation' without of course giving the notion of 'discipline' connotations of the mechanical. It is on these assumptions that Leavis tried to argue for the criticism of literature as being the central humanistic discipline. Leavis himself later praised Richards for conferring the benefit of liberation 'from the thought-frustrating spell of "form", "pure sound value", prosody and the other time-honoured quasi-critical futilities', but he had no time for Richards's pseudo-scientific psychological and semantic ambitions.

We have seen something of the opposition to the inauguration of English studies at Cambridge. With typical acerbity Leavis was later to characterize many of the early Faculty powers (Forbes and Richards excepted) as 'unchecked mediocrities'. One suspects Leavis had the classicist (and Miltonist) E. M. W. Tillyard particularly in mind. Yet Basil Willey, who was taught by Tillyard, can write of him as though he too in those heady early days was a sort of proto-Leavis:

From the start his method was to direct our attention to particular texts and passages, to make us taste their diverse qualities, comparing and distinguishing. In our essays we were to avoid mere gossip, metaphysical vapourings and woolly mysticism.

But whatever the rifts that were to develop within the Faculty and give rise to so much bad blood and to a fascinating tangle for some fair minded future historian to unravel, if that should turn out to be possible, there were at the end of the 1920s and the beginning of the 1930s three main tendencies which made the argument for literary criticism as the central humanistic discipline difficult to accept. These were first the strong Cambridge tradition which had its exemplification in the work of Whitehead and Russell (and something of a sanction, as I shall show, in the views of G. H. Hardy) that the essential nature of what constitutes a discipline was best exemplified by mathematics and logic; second the rise of Positivism, with its central contention that only the method of natural science gives us knowledge; and third the growing influence, particularly in the thirties, of a somewhat reductionist form of Marxism.

I shall illustrate the notion of the primacy of the logico-mathematical from G. H. Hardy's famous book *A Mathematician's Apology*. Although this book was not published until 1940, Hardy had had a distinguished career as a Fellow of Trinity (Russell's college also) since 1900, and it is difficult to believe that Leavis was not acquainted directly or indirectly with the ethos it represents. *A Mathematician's Apology* ought to be a *locus classicus* as a repository of a budget of misapprehensions as to the nature of humanistic discourse entertainable by an otherwise aggressively anti-Utilitarian and un-philistine number genius. In the very first paragraph we find the standard cliché 'Exposition, criticism, appreciation, is work for second-rate minds'. This view makes it impossible to do justice to the central task of the humanities which is 'to unravel the web of associations' constituted not just by works of literature in the narrow sense of poems and plays and novels, but by works of history, biography, autobiography and philosophy as well. It is significant that the only opponent of the case Hardy can conjure up (this in the Cambridge of *Scrutiny*!) is A. E. Housman, an established reputation safely associated with

Classics. This is surely indicative of the status the English studies pursued in his own University must have had in Hardy's eyes. Hardy then goes on to endorse W. J. Turner's remark that 'it is only the "highbrows" (in the unpleasant sense) who do not admire the "real swells"', by which Turner presumably meant what for him were the 'great names' of literature, Shakespeare and Dickens, whom he apparently wished to emphasize were non-highbrows. When Hardy comes to consider poetry he emphasizes that its interest lies not at all in ideas but solely in 'the beauty of the verbal pattern'. So much for Matthew Arnold's emphasis in his essays 'The Study of Poetry' and 'Wordsworth' on the importance of 'moral ideas' in the poetry that repays frequentation. Hardy insists, like Russell, on pattern, interconnectedness and generality as 'eternal' sources of 'intense emotional satisfaction'. Even a character who is in many respects the utter antithesis of Hardy and Russell, Simone Weil, can express this 'Platonistic' reverence for mathematics as the discipline of disciplines when she writes:

Unless one has exercised one's mind seriously at the gymnastic of mathematics one is incapable of precise thought, which amounts to saying that one is good for nothing.

The sense that many distinguished minds accepted logico-mathematical procedures as the paradigm for what constitutes a discipline must have disturbed Leavis. He was struck by Santayana's observation in *Winds of Doctrine* that Russell's intellect was 'at its best in subjects remote from human life', namely formal logic and mathematics, but faltered when it had to cope with concrete issues of life and mind. He endorses D. H. Lawrence's judgment that 'What ails Russell is, in matters of life and emotion, the inexperience of youth . . . It isn't that life has been too much for him, but too little'. As late as 1967 we find Leavis saying ' "English" suffers by reason of its extreme remoteness as an academic study and discipline from Mathematics: how produce and enforce the standards that determine genuine qualification?' The need is particularly pressing because creative literature itself affords an example of what Leavis in *The Great Tradition* calls 'knowledge alive with understanding', disciplined thinking which calls for apprehension by powers that are perhaps the antithesis of the mathematical.

The second tendency Leavis had to oppose was that of Positivism. The Positivists saw the method of natural science as the only source of empirical knowledge. This method consisted of the use of observation to verify or falsify whatever hypothesis was in question. The Positivists were so taken with this notion that they thought they could use it not just to mark the distinction between the scientific and the non-scientific, but the meaningful and meaningless, as in A. J. Ayer's famous book *Language, Truth and Logic* published in 1936. But the case for the view that only science can give us empirical knowledge and that all the rest is merely psychologically conditioned chat had already been wittily put in a short paper delivered in 1925 in Cambridge by the mathematical philosopher Frank Ramsey, friend of Keynes, Russell and Wittgenstein, and brother of a future Archbishop of Canterbury. Ramsey's paper was reprinted as the epilogue to his book *The Foundations of Mathematics* published in 1931. It posed the basic question in its very title 'What is there to discuss?'. Ramsey's Positivist answer could be very brief, which was fortunate as the papers delivered were limited to five minutes by a rule of the society which gathered to hear them. It was, in effect, 'nothing!' Ramsey proclaimed the Positivist credo 'There is nothing to know except science'. Ethical and aesthetic disagreements (the very centre of humanistic disputes) became merely a subject for psychological investigation as to their causes. No arguments in such subjects could be rationally vindicated. They took the absurd form of A saying 'I went to Grantchester this afternoon' and B saying 'No I didn't', and each thinking he had contradicted the other. In literary-critical disputes men, for Ramsey, are still at the stage of using such formally feeble arguments as 'Who drives fat oxen must himself be fat'. Ramsey's psychological subjectivism was adopted by F. L. Lucas, a member of the Cambridge English Faculty who cited Ramsey's paper with approval in his book *Literature and Psychology* (1951). Lucas oddly combined the view that disagreements as to the 'pleasure-value' of literature are irresolvable matters of temperament with the conviction that the 'influence-value' of literature on conduct is objectively determinable. If persons read Baudelaire constantly and keep Joyce's *Ulysses* under their pillows, it would be unwise to marry them.

What told against the Positivist view for Leavis was presumably reflection on his experience. Hadn't the writings of Eliot and others, combined with his own reading of English poetry, shown him that the acquisition, articulation and stabilization of literary preferences cannot be summed up in dismissive words about comparing notes on feelings? One talks about a poem say as something objectively there, not, it is true, in the same sense as a chair or a Cambridge college, not trippable over or pointable to in the way such physical things are, but, nevertheless, something with an existence of its own even if it depends on our minds for 'realizing' its significance. However difficult it might be to some (and repellent to others) to speak of 'analysis' and 'discipline' in this area, however inviting of misunderstanding on the part of possible friends and of dismissal on the part of entrenched foes, it was necessary to do something to vindicate his insight. He put his problem in clear unjargonic words in the preface to *Education and the University* (1943), in which he summed up his intention to formulate a discipline not of scholarly industry and academic method (as in *Literaturwissenschaft*), but of intelligence and sensibility: 'I was preoccupied with finding out how to talk to the point about poems, novels and plays, and how to promote intelligent and profitable discussion of them.' The main enemies to be combatted were the prestige of generality and misplaced demands for precise definition of terms. The wish for generality and definition come together in the aspiration to discover or lay down general norms from which the merits (or demerits) of literary works can be deduced. Leavis sees this way of trying to introduce 'discipline' into this area would be entirely misplaced. Norms could only lend a bogus objectivism to what vindicates itself on the level of phenomenological description.

René Wellek's failure to see this in the critically appreciative letter to *Scrutiny* on *Revaluation*, in which he asks Leavis to spell out the norms by which he measures every poet, prompted Leavis to reply:

By the critic of poetry I understand the complete reader: the ideal critic is the ideal reader. The reading demanded by poetry is of a different kind from the reading demanded by philosophy. I should not find it easy to define the difference satisfactorily, but Dr Wellek knows what it is and could give at least as good an account of it as I could. Philosophy, we say, is 'abstract' (thus Dr Wellek asks me to defend my position 'more abstractly'), and poetry 'concrete'. Words in poetry invite us, not to 'think about' and judge but to 'feel into' or 'become'—to realize a complex experience that is given in the words. They demand, not merely a fuller bodied response, but a completer responsiveness—a kind of responsiveness that is incompatible with the judicial, one-eye-on-the-standard approach suggested by Dr Wellek's phrase: 'your "norm" by which you measure every poet.' The critic—the reader of poetry—is indeed concerned with evaluation, but to figure him as measuring with a norm which he brings up to the object and applies from the outside is to misrepresent the process. The critic's aim is, first, to realize as sensitively and completely as possible this or that which claims his attention; and a certain valuing is implicit in the realizing . . .

Leavis continues:

In making value-judgements (and judgements as to significance), implicitly or explicitly, he does so out of that completeness of possession and with that fullness of response. He doesn't ask, 'How does this accord with these specifications of goodness in poetry?'; he aims to make fully conscious and articulate the immediate sense of value that 'places' the poem.

Leavis is careful to insist that the type of analysis of poetry proposed should be completely dissociated from all notions of 'murdering to dissect'. There is no purely external 'apparatus' which can be handed over, so that in a kind of Baconian 'levelling of wits' any fool can use it. There can be nothing in the nature of 'proof' or 'laboratory demonstration'. Even 'the best critical terms and concepts . . . will be inadequate to the varied complexities with which the critic has to deal', for the critic is concerned with the particular use of assonance, say, not with subsuming an instance under the general classification 'assonance' in order to deduce some further value property—'a certain valuing is implicit in the realizing'. Leavis developed an extraordinary skill at naming the nexus of associations called up in his mind by a particular passage of poetry and at articulating an appropriate network of reflection around it. His constant concern was 'the appropriate directing of attention upon poetry' so that the poetry is 'apperceived' or taken into the mind in such a way as to connect up with a matrix of relevant connections. Perhaps the best account of the process is to be found in the essays entitled 'Judgment and Analysis: Notes in the Analysis of Poetry' originally published in *Scrutiny* for 1945 and reprinted in *The Living Principle* (1975). Just as the poet in his poem presents us with a situation in such a way that his 'presenting involves an *attitude towards*, an element of disinterested valuation of what is presented' so the critic performs a second valuational act or 'placing' on this already existent and artistically objectified primary one. This second act is an analysis of the critic's own experience of the poem and in performing it the critic must, in Leavis's words, 'while keeping it alive and immediately present as experience, treat it in some sense as an object'. We are not just making autobiographical remarks about our feelings, then, as Frank Ramsey supposed, but are performing the complex act of talking about objects to which those feelings are directed, objects which, however, do not exist independently of those feelings and objects which have themselves been created originally out of a combination of presentations and implicit valuations by the poets themselves. Leavis, then, is a Formalist in so far as all his discussions (at their best) are tied to the particular tone and texture of actual works, but he is a moralist in that there is a substantive concern with human attitudes constantly present in those discussions.

In fact it can reasonably be claimed that what Leavis provided was a way of grappling with moral problems without commitment to discredited substantive ideologies on the one hand, and without the vacuousness of the meta-ethical approaches which had begun to engross moral philosophy itself on the other. In short, it filled the gap left for the ethical sensibility by Positivists like Ramsey and Ayer. That sensibility was given free play in the rich pastures of imaginative literature, a storehouse of non-trivial examples of morally perplexing situations with implicit valuations already built into the way they were actually presented. At the same time Leavis's own tough-mindedness, his iconoclasm towards the grandiose ambitions of the literary historians of the past, and towards any hint of religious and metaphysical bombinations 'about' literature as opposed to an engagement 'with' literature, meant that his practice had a curious parallel to that of the Positivists with their deflation of empty edification in morals and pretentious metaphysics in speculation. Leavis, too, importantly shared the Positivist scepticism about the transcendental claims of religion. In the 1945–55 period the (in some ways opposed, in some ways parallel), twin confluences of Positivism and of Leavis's criticism met in a hard headed concern to force people to spell out the values of whatever claims they were making in the presence of particular examples. Leavis's influence was certainly at its height in that post-war decade.

The third tendency Leavis had to oppose was the Marxism that was growing more and more popular among intellectuals in the 1930s. Leavis's reaction against it is well exemplified in his review of Trotsky's *Literature and Revolution*. This was entitled 'Under Which King, Bezonian?' and appeared as an editorial to the third number of the first volume of *Scrutiny* in December 1932. The title is a happy allusion to the impudent *bragadocchio* of Pistol, when, in Act V scene 4 of *Henry IV Part Two* he teases Shallow (who claims authority as a Justice under the King, not knowing that Henry IV had died) with the challenge:

Under which king, Bezonian? Speak or die.

Leavis opens by saying that it would be very innocent of us to be surprised by the frequency with which we are asked to 'show our colours'. If the elusive Santayana himself can resort to such a formulation, what can we expect from the devotees of orthodoxy? As far as Marxism is concerned, Leavis is very witty about the problem of discovering 'what precisely orthodoxy is'. Even the Cambridge economist Maurice Dobb, 'whom Mr Eliot singles out for commendation', is not 'very lucid'. But on one thing Leavis is clear. The dogma of 'the priority of economic conditions' must be rejected as hostile to the whole ethos of the *Scrutiny* enterprise, an enterprise which is incompatible with the notion that the free intelligence of man is wholly determined by material forces beyond its grasp, indeed the living falsification of such a notion. Whether Marx himself constantly held such a view is, of course, moot. A recent commentator on Marx and literature, S. Prawer, recognizes that Marx seems to hold such a position in his famous preface to *A Contribution to the Critique of Political Economy*, but Engels in his equally famous letter to Bloch replaced the notion of one-way causality by a notion of dialectical interaction which is less offensive at the price of being more vacuous.

Leavis sees Trotsky himself, 'the Marxist excommunicate', as 'a cultivated as well as an unusually intelligent man', who recognizes that there is much more to 'culture' than something merely class-conditioned. Indeed, despite 'the familiar air of scientific rigour' where scientific rigour of the kind we associate with physics and mathematics is impossible, Trotsky recognizes that it is the autonomous striving towards a truly human culture which makes man the species being he is. Man is neither a mere epiphenomenon of economic forces nor an aspirer to pure science and nothing else. But an advocate of a truly human culture like Trotsky who can 'cheerfully contemplate fifty years of revolutionary warfare' is, for Leavis, tainted by the shallow optimism we associate with H. G. Wells at his worst. Leavis shares Trotsky's view that 'the development of Art is the highest test of the vitality and significance of each epoch', but he is much less confident that the gigantic industrialized societies of the future, as conceived by Trotsky, will produce art of the quality left us by those creative minorities within the agrarian societies of the past, which did not lose fructifying contact with the agricultural rhythms that were the material 'base' of their lives. Leavis's deploring of the readiness of writers to line up in rival camps as having more to do with ego and with chic than with thinking, and his cutting irony at 'the ready development of antagonisms among those whose differences are inessential' have lost nothing of their force and relevance. Though he may be guilty of idealizing the past, he may be correct in undercutting Marxism by suggesting that it could itself be an epiphenomenon of the situation it purports to be uniquely able to explain, somewhat in the way that Karl Kraus undercut psychoanalysis:

Class of the kind that can justify talk about 'class culture' has long been extinct. (And, it might be added, when there was such 'class culture' it was much more than merely of the class.) The process of civilization that produced among other things, the Marxian dogma, and makes it plausible, has made the cultural difference between the 'classes' inessential.

Leavis saw the function of *Scrutiny* in this connection as being to insist on the importance of its own task of providing a platform for the kind of 'disinterested' criticism of literature, the intense engagement without *parti pris*, which was not able to find an outlet elsewhere. Any further 'more immediate engaging upon the world of practice' he felt to lie within the world of education in particular, rather than with any grandiose schemes for economic and political revolution in society at large.

It ought to be emphasized that it was not just Marxist demands for 'showing one's colours' that Leavis rejected. The 1940s and early 1950s also saw a revival of what might be called neo-Christianity. The C. S. Lewis–Charles Williams circle at Oxford developed their distinctive version of neo-Christian apologetic. Elsewhere the now Anglican Eliot's poetry, particularly *Ash Wednesday* and *Four Quartets* played its role. Auden had been converted to a sort of Kierkegaardian Christianity from his flirtation with Marx and Freud. I am old enough to remember coming across Brother George Every's little book *Poetry and Personal Responsibility*, a Student Christian Movement publication, being sold on a stall at a school discussion on religion around 1949–50. Ronald Hayman is perhaps right to call Leavis's attack on this book 'of little interest today', and to regret the inclusion of Leavis's review of it in *The Common Pursuit* at the expense of better material. Nevertheless in so far as the moral substance of ideologies (as opposed to their scientific pretentions) is concerned, Christianity is infinitely more important than

Marxism, which, in so far as it makes moral judgments (whatever Marx's overt disclaimers about doing this) can even be regarded as a Christian heresy. It remains of interest, therefore, to see what Leavis's literary-critical stance *vis-à-vis* Christian claims is. Brother Every had fallen into a not unnatural, though, in the case of Leavis, rather a crass mistake. He had assumed that because Leavis did not commit himself in the abstract to a substantive ideological position he must be an aesthete, or, in Marxist parlance, a 'Formalist'. He did not see that if we are to call Leavis a 'Formalist', it must be with the qualification that his Formalism can encompass a consideration of the ethical content internal to (or 'realized' in) the works of art he is discussing, and is no pure Formalism of patterns and textures. Indeed Leavis's criticism of the work of Charles Williams, a poet and critic enjoying something of a vogue in certain circles at that time, and praised by Every, is essentially an ethical one:

if you approach as a literary critic, unstiffened by the determination to 'discriminate Christianly', or if you approach merely with ordinary sensitiveness and good sense, you can hardly fail to see that Williams' preoccupation with the 'horror of evil' is evidence of an arrest at the schoolboy (and -girl) stage rather than of spiritual maturity, and that his dealings in 'myth', mystery, the occult and the supernatural belong essentially to the ethos of the thriller. To pass off his writings as spiritually edifying is to promote the opposite of spiritual health.

Leavis's dismissal of 'attitudinizing and gesturing' about causes that one feels important will never lose its timelessness; and the same is true of his warning that those who propagate a sense that 'to feel vaguely excited and impressed is to have grappled with serious problems' will only in the end damage the doctrine they purport to be defending. The 'critical examination' performed even in the cause of some doctrine must bear internally within itself evidence of the rightness and delicacy of the critic's responses to the work he is examining. When that delicacy is absent, no asseveration of orthodoxy, of whatever kind, can make up for it.

IV. LEAVIS'S NEW HISTORY OF
ENGLISH POETRY

The art of poetry centrally engaged the interest of the early
Leavis. Later his emphasis was to shift more to prose fiction.
As we have seen in our account of his later dispute with F. W.
Bateson he had come to reject literary history in the old sense,
what we might call 'expository' history. He objected to
Oliver Elton's *Survey of English Literature*, for example,
because 'there is not a paragraph of criticism in all the six
volumes'. The only kind of literary history possible for
Leavis now was 'critical' history, a history 'objective' not
through any purported neutrality, but through the dis-
interestedly sincere discussion of particular examples in the
light of the reactions of a sensibility newly alerted by the
achievement of T. S. Eliot to the possibilities of poetic
expression inherent in the English language. The seminal
works *New Bearings in English Poetry* (1932) and *Revaluation*
(1936) are literary history of this 'critical' kind.

Leavis's reaction against literary history in the old sense has
a strong affinity with Nietzsche's reaction in his essay 'The
Use and Abuse of History' against the idea that a neutralist
academic objectivity is possible in history proper. Such inert
history is, for Nietzsche, the enemy of life. When we contemplate the 'classic' and the 'rare' in the past, it is in order to
hearten us for equivalent achievement in the present, not in
order to escape to some Palladium, or fortress of safe classi-
cism from which we can scorn all living growth. A purely
'internal culture' unrelated to the 'external barbarism'
around us is no good and only makes us more firmly a part
of that 'external barbarism' ourselves. A true objectivity with
regard to the achievements of the past is reached only by an
intimate personal engagement with the content and form of
the works themselves, not by a 'historicist' preoccupation
with their sources and antecedents in the history of the life
and times of their authors. Moreover, declares Nietzsche:
'*You can explain the past only by what is most powerful in the
present*'.

These words might well have been made the motto of *New
Bearings in English Poetry* and *Revaluation*. In both books it is

31

conspicuously the influence of Eliot which figures as the example of 'what is most powerful in the present' and underwrites the whole approach. What might well be called Leavis's 'sober Nietzscheanism' ('we didn't need Nietzsche to tell us to live dangerously; there is no other way of living') is nicely brought out in the later essay 'Eliot's Axe to Grind' in *English Literature in our Time and the University* (1969). In it Leavis defends the stimulatory value of Eliot's criticism of the Metaphysical poets against J. B. Leishman's claim that it was vitiated because Eliot had an 'axe to grind' and worked from too limited a knowledge of the poets. For Leavis this is somewhat like saying that Shakespeare did not know enough about classical antiquity to write Roman plays. He retorts that Eliot 'knew enough for his purpose'. We might compare Nietzsche's remark: 'The knowledge of the past is desired only for the service of the future and the present, not to weaken the present or undermine a living future'. Eliot for Leavis, does not give us 'inert' knowledge about the seventeenth century which we can passively take over, as if it were 'certified factual knowledge'. He invites collaborative assent (or dissent) to observations which arise from what might paradoxically be called an 'interested disinterestedness' as opposed to the purely scholarly and, as Leavis sees it, less challenging 'disinterestedness' of a Leishman. Leavis does not think Eliot's formula of 'felt thought' has worn well as a characterization of Donne, but he defends the notion of 'the dissociation of sensibility' as sensitizing us to the important distinction between the ability to turn our interests 'into poetry' and 'not merely meditate on them poetically' in Eliot's phrase.

The distinction is central for Leavis. He is ruthless in spotting 'the will to poetry' masquerading as the real thing, as in Edith Sitwell's writing 'emotionally, and with characteristic afflatus, about Christ'. One only wishes that Leavis himself had had the energy to go on sorting out the examples of 'the will to poetry' from the genuine article in more recent writers. And it is not always just the false afflatus which he condemns. The sort of 'objectivist' poetry which trusts to the negative virtues of avoiding such afflatus was also touched on by Leavis in his review of Pound's *Active Anthology* in

1933, when he wrote that 'the inadequate conception of "technique"' was the most charitable explanation of 'the inclusion, for instance, of so much nullity by Mr Louis Zukofsky'. Leavis was unconvinced by the claims made for the dry poetry of Marianne Moore.

Both *New Bearings* and *Revaluation* raise difficult issues which now need surveying. Discounting the point as to whether Leavis exaggerates his own part in getting Eliot's poetic achievement (and the nature of the modern poetic achievement in general) recognized, there is, first, the question as to whether his account of the nature of that achievement in *New Bearings* is sufficiently coherent. Secondly there is the often repeated contention that Leavis's methods are only adapted to doing justice to the short poem of some intellectual complexity. Thirdly there is the issue of whether some of Leavis's own re-writing of literary history, in particular his assessment of Milton and his view of Pope as a continuer of metaphysical wit, are not by now, naturally enough, in need of some revaluation themselves.

Leavis begins *New Bearings* by arguing that 'contemporary intelligence' goes into fields other than poetry. Perhaps Leavis has mathematics, natural science and economics in mind. Poetry since the nineteenth century has been seen as a dream escape composed by one who is

The idle singer of an empty day.

Indeed Eliot's particular achievement has resulted from his gift for putting the full and free play of his intelligence at the service of his poetry, so that all his interests as a mature adult can enter that poetry through a working together, or synergy, of his interest in experience and his interest in words. Leavis, it is too seldom noticed, is not completely dismissive of 'a poetry of withdrawal' and does make fine discriminations between examples of it. He is particularly good on the fruitfulness of the tension between Yeats's worldly shrewdness and energy and his attraction to reverie, and on the link between enchantment and disenchantment in De la Mare. Hardy's work does not belong to the poetry of day dreams, but Leavis shrewdly sees the 'modern thought' that engrossed

33

him as comfortably 'Victorian' in its certitudes rather than really modern, even if those certitudes were bleakly pessimistic. Eliot's 'modernism' involves the invention of techniques 'that shall be adequate to the ways of feeling, or modes of experience, of adult sensitive moderns'. I want now to consider the coherence of Leavis's account of this 'modernism'.

He proposes a multiplicity of criteria for it. The first is the defiance of 'the traditional canon of seriousness'. The second is the revolt against the notion of the intrinsically 'poetical'. The third is a use of 'audacities of transition and psychological notation, such as are forbidden to the novelist' and which enable the poet to project himself into 'a comprehensive and representative human consciousness'. The fourth is the closeness of the poet's own work to the idiom of 'his own speech', as we shall see perhaps the most ambiguously troublesome criterion of all. The fifth (perhaps bound up with the third) is the use of a disjointed allusiveness arising from the complexity of an educated man's relation to the past. The sixth is the use of 'musical' as opposed to 'narrative' organization. Leavis never makes it sufficiently clear, perhaps, whether any one of these six criteria is a sufficient condition for the presence of a 'modernity' with a kinship to Eliot's distinctive achievement. He may, indeed, intend to suggest that Eliot's distinctiveness lies in the fact that his work embodies all six criteria. As far as Leavis's re-writing of the history of English poetry in the light of his strong reaction to Eliot's achievement goes (and this applies very much to *Revaluation* as well as to *New Bearings*), it is the fourth criterion concerning idiom or diction, namely the demand for the closeness of the poet's own work to the idiom of 'his own speech' which is both the most important and which gives the most trouble.

The trouble arises because Leavis does not seem enough aware of the fact that he oscillates between a rather narrow interpretation of his fourth criterion (namely that the 'poetic voice' should be demonstrably close to that of the poet's conversation with his contemporaries, 'Language such as men do use', in Ben Jonson's words) and a rather wider interpretation of it which sanctions a past poet's use of a 'lofty and formal decorum' which no modern poet could use, but

34

which a modern reader 'should have no difficulty in living into'. The first interpretation is precise, but exclusive. The second interpretation would be flexible enough to include passages in *Paradise Lost* and *The Prelude*, which one assumes that the first interpretation would exclude. Leavis is using the first interpretation when he claims that the 'staple idiom and movement' of Eliot's own poetry 'derive immediately from modern speech' and when he writes in *Revaluation* that Donne gives us the 'utterance, movement and intonation' of 'the talking voice' and that his Satire III has 'a natural speaking stress and intonation' and shows a remarkable 'mimetic flexibility' which in 'a consummately managed verse' can 'exploit the strength of spoken English'. He is using the second interpretation when in the Pope essay in *Revaluation* he speaks of Pope's decorum as 'natural because it was sanctioned by contemporary convention'.

Of course Leavis is right to protest in *The Common Pursuit* against Tillyard's travestying his views into the claim that the 'language of small talk' is 'the basis of all good poetry'. But for Leavis to go on to say that he never complained 'that Milton did not write *Paradise Lost* in the style of Shakespeare', or (however different this is) 'in a conversational style' or 'the' tone of ordinary speech', as he does in his reply to Tillyard in *The Common Pursuit* in the essay 'In Defence of Milton', is to be disingenuous. Of course Leavis never made precisely those claims, but they are not (unlike the remark about 'small talk') unwarranted distortions of the contrast in *Revaluation* between the 'Shakespearean life' of parts of *Comus* and 'the laboured, pedantic artifice' of *Paradise Lost* with its remoteness 'from any English that was ever spoken' and its 'wearying deadness', even when it is at its most brilliant, 'to the ear that appreciates Shakespeare'. On the wider interpretation of Leavis's fourth criterion it could be claimed that *Paradise Lost* has a decorum which may indeed not have been very far from the living voice of John Milton, and which though (to borrow Leavis's own phrasing from his account of Pope in *Revaluation*) 'so lofty and formal' that no modern poet could adopt it successfully, is nevertheless of a type that 'the modern reader should have no difficulty living into'. The questions raised by the debate about Milton's style are too complex to examine in detail in a study devoted to Leavis himself, but it is necessary to say something about them. The controversy, as Christopher Ricks has pointed out in his book *Milton's Grand Style*, is a triangular one. There is, on the one hand, Leavis's clash with C. S. Lewis, who claims to see Milton's verse as Leavis does, but to reject Leavis's criteria, in short to admire the very same qualities in the poetry that Leavis dislikes. Then there is the position of Ricks himself who, rightly I think, sees *Paradise Lost* as having more variety than either Leavis or Lewis allows, and who, sharing Leavis's demand that poetry should not employ an empty eloquence that disarms attention, but should, on the contrary, call for the closest scrutiny, claims that much of *Paradise Lost* asks for and rewards the most minute attention. What can certainly be claimed for Leavis is that he allows no one to assent to the value of Milton merely conventionally, on the grounds of inert tradition.

One of the puzzling elements in Leavis's rejection of Milton is Leavis's own turning away from a Puritan moral ethos of 'decency' (with an almost Laurentian concern to celebrate the primal mysteries of sexual love) to endorse the interest of the work of a court wit like Carew with its affirmation of libertine sensuousness. This is hard to square with Leavis's later asseveration: 'I don't believe in any "literary values", and you won't find me talking about them; the judgments the literary critic is concerned with are judgments about life.' Leavis finds the great literary exemplar of Puritanism (perhaps he ought more precisely to be called a sectary as R. L. Greaves suggests) in Bunyan, perhaps because of the more experiential quality of Bunyan's expression of his religious interests, what R. L. Greaves calls the Lutheran concern with the wrath–grace dichotomy, as opposed to the Calvinist concern with 'the divine will and omnipotence'. In Luther's commentary on *Galatians*, which we know from *Grace Abounding* that Bunyan read and was influenced by, there is a passage (quoted by Greaves) which states that 'true Christian divinity . . . commandeth us not to search out the nature of God . . .' saying that there is 'nothing more dangerous than to wander with curious speculations in heaven, and there to search out God in his incomprehensible power, wisdom and Majesty'.

Milton in his portrayal of the fall of Satan and of God the Father (particular with the latter's speech in Book III of *Paradise Lost*) boldly ignored Luther's warning and embarked on

> Things unattempted yet in prose or rhyme.

Nevertheless Leavis's contention that Milton was 'ludicrously unqualified' to undertake a poetic theodicy, in that he possessed 'character rather than intelligence', raises more complex issues than the critic seems prepared to consider, and makes one wonder how far Leavis himself had really pondered the nature of such an enterprise in terms of the expectations and beliefs of a seventeenth century Christian. Leavis's view that Milton was tactless and clumsy in the way he handled his material seems, for example, difficult to reconcile with the fact that an intelligent contemporary of Milton's (and one whom Leavis greatly admires, Andrew Marvell) could write of *Paradise Lost*

> Thou hast not missed one thought that could be fit.
> And all that was improper dost omit.

A further reason for Leavis's inability to do justice to *Paradise Lost* may lie in the fact that the kind of intense local scrutiny which works for a Donne or Herbert lyric may not be appropriate for a poem of such length. The notion that 'the whole organism is present in the part' in longer works is a matter of faith rather than vindicated assumption. True, it seems to work with much of the 'organic' Shakespeare (any of whose great tragedies Leavis sees as 'an incomparably better whole than *Paradise Lost*'), but isn't the drama, as a genre, traditionally and by definition more tightly knit than the epic? We shall meet this problem again in connection with the criticism of the novel. One feels that Leavis's repugnance to the theological material intrinsic to the poem may lie behind his unwillingness to concede that he has not done justice to the narrative and ideological problems involved in the architectonic of *Paradise Lost*, an architectonic beside which modern long poems such as the *Cantos* and *Paterson* emerge as collections of single passages rather than unified poems at all. Sometimes one wonders if some of the hostility aroused by a classicizing critic like Tillyard was not displaced on to Milton himself. At one point in *The Common Pursuit* Leavis turns round and defends 'that unique heroic figure', with whom he is nevertheless so deeply out of sympathy, against his defender, Tillyard.

One figure with whom Leavis is importantly engaged in *New Bearings* and later is Gerard Manley Hopkins. Later studies of Hopkins have tended to stress his links with his own period and the artifice of his language as opposed to its closeness to spoken idiom. We know from his letters that Hopkins greatly admired the irregular rhythm of Milton's *Samson Agonistes*, a work which Leavis has always regarded as overrated. Nevertheless the late publication of Hopkins's poetry (it did not appear till 1918) meant that Leavis's account was one of the earliest original and important contributions to its appreciation. Leavis emphasized its contrast with the dream world of many of the Victorians, and also with the cult of mellifluous musicality associated with Tennyson. Hopkins's neglect and the misunderstandings of Bridges could with some justice be attributed to the too narrow neo-classicism fostered by that sense of superiority given by the cultivation of Latin and Greek, that 'trade in classic niceties' which Leavis always saw as an enemy. Hopkins's view that 'the poetical language of an age should be the current language heightened', and his rejection of archaisms was exactly the one Leavis also had to champion in his evaluation of Eliot's distinctive achievement. At the same time Hopkins's linguistic experiments were not the mere exuberance of a Browning, but put to the service, notably in 'The Wreck of the Deutschland', of delicate moral apprehensions. There are also two excellent essays on Hopkins in *The Common Pursuit*. Leavis's lecture to The Hopkins Society in 1971 makes some qualifications. In it he says he never found 'The Windhover' successful (there is no indication in *New Bearings* that he thought it a failure and it is commended in *The Common Pursuit*) and he reiterates his praise for the un-Swinburnian basically 'traditional' art of 'The Wreck of the Deutschland'. He claims Eliot to be 'very much the greater poet', but says that Hopkins, as man and personality, rouses his 'respect, admiration and affection', perhaps because, as he says in his conclusion, 'Hopkins, in a wholly unpejorative sense, was simple', a judgment some might, indeed, make of Leavis himself.

On Shakespeare Leavis has not offered a great deal in quantity, and admirers (or ex-admirers?) of Leavis's work have even spoken of *'Scrutiny's* failure with Shakespeare'. Nevertheless the work he has given us here makes up for its sparseness by its quality. There is a fine analysis of a Macbeth soliloquy in *Education and the University*, and, in *The Common Pursuit*, a suggestive interpretation of *Othello* (which, however, probably overreacts against the romanticizing of Othello's character), a thoughtful look at *Measure for Measure*, and a helpful piece on the late plays. Leavis also gives us in the essay 'Tragedy and the "Medium" ' an excellent essay on tragedy which stresses the element of exaltation aroused by certain tragedies and the concomitant 'escape from all attitudes of self-assertion', coupled with a recognition of positive value that avoids pessimism on the one hand and optimism on the other. The essay is yet another illustration of what I have called Leavis's 'sober Nietzscheanism'. Among modern poets Yeats (whom he always nevertheless assiduously read) does not really receive his due in terms of analysis, despite Leavis's excellent account of the Byzantium poems and his recognition of the poet's greatness, particularly in *The Tower*. However, the Leavisian approach rightly challenges that kind of pure exegesis which assumes proprietorial rights, so to speak, over the poet and from which both Yeats and Blake have suffered. Leavis's refusal to accord greatness to Auden, his unwillingness to concede more than a clever intelligence and a fluency with words and concepts, is very much a matter of controversy.

V. THE NOVEL: THE GREAT TRADITION

In 'How to Teach Reading', first published as a reply to Ezra Pound's pamphlet *How to Read*, and reprinted as an appendix to *Education and the University*, Leavis admits that all the exemplifying in the pamphlet 'has been from poetry', but goes on to claim that prose 'demands the same approach' while conceding that it 'admits it far less readily'. Novels, indeed, raise once again the problem of the failure of the Leavisian approach to deal as happily with questions of architectonic as it does with that of 'local life', and, indeed, compound it, as a long poem is not supposed to fall beneath a certain minimum distinction of style even in 'flat' passages while, as Leavis acknowledges, 'a page of a novel that is as a whole significant may appear undistinguished or even poor'. Nevertheless Leavis goes on to say:

Yet though the devising and applying of a critical technique may be found difficult in the case of prose-literature it should not . . . be impossible. Out of a School of English that provided the training suggested here might come, not only a real literary criticism of Shakespeare, but a beginning in the criticism of the novel.

A rueful note appended in 1943 adds:

I leave here these light-hearted sentences about the 'criticism of the novel' as they stood. Actually, nothing helpful in respect of that problem can be said briefly. I hope to bring out before long in collaboration with Q. D. Leavis a book that deals with the grounds and methods of the critical study of novels.

This work, like the announced article on Conrad entitled *Conrad, the Soul and the Universe* mentioned in *The Great Tradition*, remains one of the great unwritten works of criticism. But at least *The Great Tradition* includes some penetrating reflections on the nature of Conrad's work. What it certainly does not do is demonstrate that 'the grounds and methods of the critical study of novels' are the same as those of the critical study of complex lyric poems. A lyric poem can be held in the mind and so surveyed as a complete self-contained whole. One sometimes wonders whether Leavis's reference to Lawrence's novels as 'dramatic poems' in *D. H. Lawrence: Novelist* is not an attempt to stake the struggle on a name, but, in any case, it involves a recognition of the *difference* between Lawrence's novels and, for the most part, the novels dealt with in *The Great Tradition*.

In *The Great Tradition* itself, as John Killham has pointed out in an article in *The British Journal of Aesthetics* for January 1965, the term 'concreteness' does not always very happily fit the 'patterned', more 'fabular' novel of the type of *Hard Times*. He sees Leavis as equivocating on the term. Sometimes it evokes verisimilitude, as when applied to the portrayal of Gwendolen Harleth in *Daniel Deronda*, and sometimes it evokes a 'realism' of moral insight on the part of the author which is compatible with a fabular violation of verisimilitude. Leavis, for him, oscillates between the notion of 'felt life' as connectible with the author's life-experience and ultimately rooted in his personal problems, and the more 'Horatian' notion of it as the artist's gift for transporting his readers into 'well-imagined situations'. The term 'realization' also lends itself to ambiguities here in the analysis of both prose and poetry. Indeed in the essay 'Reality and Sincerity' Leavis had even hazarded the view that 'It is a case in which we know from the art what the man was like' after discussing Hardy's 'After a Journey', a remark looking particularly ironic in the light of the revelations of the second volume of Gittings's biography. Killham indeed poses the difficult question of the coherence of Leavis's claims for the study of English literature which arises if we regard his approach as being a discipline. After claiming that in *Education and the University*, the earlier book, 'one finds rehearsed the whole argument of *The Great Tradition*, complete with self-contradictions', Killham writes:

we are told on the one hand that: 'What we are concerned with in analysis are always matters of complex verbal organization,' and on the other that not merely the training of the sensibility but 'the equipping of the student against the snares of "technique" ' is the aim of literary education. It is hard to see, on the face of it, that these ends are not mutually exclusive.

Killham sees it as an objection to Leavis that he uses the term 'concreteness' so indiscriminately that it becomes 'nothing more than an index of its user's own sensibility'. I would say on the contrary that the Leavisian approach is defensible here. Killham himself seems to be hoping for some by-passing or short circuiting of the individual sensibility by the critical 'method' adopted. He is guilty of an *ignoratio elenchi*, or refutation of a view not actually advanced by his opponent. It is Leavis's very contention that in this area we have to combine the apparently dichotomous notions of discipline and personal sensibility. It is not self-contradictory to suppose that we can at the same time train the sensibility and warn against the snares of technique. If the use of a term reveals the sensibility of the user (rather than being purely neutral and external to it) that is the very thing the Leavisian approach desiderates. But though I would reject Killham's case against this approach, I do think his essay brings out some of the particular difficulties of that approach as far as the art of the novel is concerned.

Tolstoy, surely one of Leavis's touchstones, once wrote in his diary:

There is a novelist's poetry: (1) in the interest of the arrangement of occurrences . . . (2) in the presentation of manners on an historic background . . . (3) in the beauty and gaiety of a situation . . . (4) in people's characters.

This novelist's 'poetry' calls for a distinctive approach, an approach that cannot dispense with a concern for probability, the management of the passage of time, the portrayal of manners, the 'situating' of a diversity of characters, the sense of where to begin and end a narrative and sub-narrative, the use of illuminating incident, the nature of 'convincing' character psychology, all the kinds of thing dealt with in a book like, say, Edith Wharton's *The Writing of Fiction*. In fact a work like *The Great Tradition* has to deal with them too and does not and cannot contain the type of analysis with which Leavis approached lyric poems such as Hardy's 'After a Journey' or Arnold's sonnet on Shakespeare. It is here that there is something of the incoherence which Killham discerned. Leavis, in parallel with the L. C. Knights rejection of the 'character' approach to Shakespeare, disclaims a concern with the creation of 'delightful characters' for its own sake, and with irrelevant 'chaotic liveliness'. So far, so good, but there are further overtones of a theoretical rejection of 'character' with which the actual practice in *The Great Tradition* conflicts.

Edith Wharton once remarked that the distinction between the novel and the short story turns on the fact that 'the *test* of the novel is that its people should be *alive*' because 'No subject in itself, however fruitful, appears to be able to keep the novel alive; only the characters in it can.' The novel was called 'a system of biographies' by the Russian poet Mandelstam. Whatever the theoretical disclaimers at the outset, there is much in *The Great Tradition* which is, in fact, perfectly compatible with both these remarks. Leavis, like any naturally engaged reader of *Middlemarch*, has moments when he would like to break Rosamond Vincy's graceful neck. He finds George Eliot's 'sheer informedness about society' impressive as 'knowledge alive with understanding' and compares her 'profound psychological analysis' with that of Tolstoy. Leavis even suspects 'an actual historical person' lies behind Conrad's portrayal of Peter Ivanych in *Under Western Eyes*, and yet there is no indication that such a suspicion points to a flaw in the 'art' of the book, rather the comment seems to register as a tribute to Conrad's powers of character portrayal. Leavis much prefers the early James novels (notably *The Bostonians* and *The Portrait of a Lady*) to the later James, and acknowledges that these books possess 'overt attractions that might seem to qualify them for popularity', by which one assumes he means convincing characters and striking scenes. Even though it is true that he speaks of the vitality of *The Portrait of a Lady* as having nothing of 'irrelevant "life"' about it, as being 'wholly of art' yet, within that art, he sees James as achieving some remarkable 'psychological analysis', particularly in *The Bostonians*.

The novel is the art form which least lends itself to the 'dehumanization of art' spoken of by Ortega y Gasset who also, by the way, thought that character and atmosphere were of primary importance within it. It is not surprising then that explicitly de-naturalizing and de-humanizing schools of criticism, notably Structuralism, should find 'character' particularly difficult to deal with. Jonathan Culler, a recent sympathetic, if critical, expositor of Structuralism, puts the issue as follows on p. 230 of his *Structuralist Poetics*:

Character is the major aspect of the novel to which structuralism has paid least attention. . . . Stress on the inter-personal and conventional systems which traverse the individual, which make him a space in which forces and events meet rather than an individuated essence, leads to a rejection of the prevalent conception of character in the novel: that the most successful and 'living' characters are richly delineated autonomous wholes, clearly distinguished from others by physical and psychological characteristics.

It is to its honour that, for all his caveats about the 'character' approach, the whole thrust of Leavis's criticism leads to the rejection of the de-naturalization and de-humanization of one of the greatest forms and forces for moral exploration and understanding invented by man, and one unknown to classical antiquity—the novel. *The Great Tradition* emphasizes how important for humanity's moral development the right understanding and right prizing of that invention are.

The standard objection to *The Great Tradition* on its appearance was that it was too narrow, too uncatholic. The objection was wittily anticipated by Leavis himself when, on the opening page, he (rightly) prophesied that people would attribute to him the view that 'except Jane Austen, George Eliot, James and Conrad, there are no novelists in English worth reading'. I read the book as an undergraduate at Oxford in the early 1950s when the English syllabus still ended in 1832 (except for an optional paper), and when it was possible to take the examination papers without doing a single essay on a novelist (as, in fact, I did) though, of course, one was expected to read some. My tutor, F.W. Bateson, held the view that the novel (except as a vehicle of satire) was intrinsically inferior to poetry as a genre, and later gave it witty expression in a lecture entitled 'The Novel's Original Sin' (printed in his *Essays in Critical Dissent*) in which one finds something of the classicist's looking down on the novel as a form, combined with an odd echo of the old Evangelical objection to fiction as lying and time-wasting, in short, as an 'addiction'. For me (and I suspect for many others) *The Great Tradition* did not close doors (as C. S. Lewis has accused the Leavis-type criticism of doing), but opened them. It guided me to a diversity of riches I don't think I would have discovered for myself, while at the same time giving me some sort of bearings, *points de repère*, among that diversity. The kind of concern with George Eliot, James and Conrad that has entered so much published criticism in the three decades since the book was published, and the way in which these authors have figured in fiction courses taught in new universities surely owe an incalculable amount to *The Great Tradition*.

The positive achievement is a magnificent one and can never be taken away from Leavis. To take one instance. George Eliot's defects had commonly been related to over-intellectualism. With great finesse Leavis brought out in his analysis of her work how they were really bound up with a kind of over-emotionalism. But, of course, there are reservations to be made about Leavis as a critic of prose fiction. He was undoubtedly too dismissive of both Proust and Mann. One suspects he was too much influenced by the fact that the first was taken up by Clive Bell and Bloomsbury, and that both were treated somewhat critically by D. H. Lawrence. He has never engaged at any length with Dostoevsky or Chekhov. He is unsatisfactory on many aspects of Bunyan (his essay on *The Pilgrim's Progress* in *Anna Karenina and Other Essays* is disappointing and plays down the difficulties raised by Bunyan's religious fanaticism), on American literature outside James, on Dickens and on Lawrence himself, in the latter case because of over-partisanship. The case of Dickens is an interesting one. In *The Great Tradition* he is frankly dismissed as no more than 'a great entertainer', who 'had for the most part no profounder responsibility as a creative artist than this description suggests' except in the one work *Hard Times*. He would be good family reading if the habit of family reading still persisted, but 'The adult mind doesn't as a rule find in Dickens a challenge to an unusual and sustained seriousness'. *Hard Times* is exempted because its fable embodies a moral indictment of the 'Benthamism' which Leavis sees as the enemy of life in our own time as well as during the nineteenth century. Yet with the appearance of *Dickens the Novelist* in 1970, a work of joint authorship with Queenie Leavis who made distinguished contributions to it, all this was modified. Of course it is perfectly legitimate that critics should change their minds (Musil once said he had done so several times about Rilke and was still undecided!), but at least they should explicitly acknowledge the fact. It was disingenuous, to say the least, to write a preface to *Dickens the Novelist* which referred disparagingly to those who 'tell us with the familiar easy assurance that Dickens of course was a genius, but that his line was entertainment' without at least acknowledging that this was the very same view that *Fiction and the Reading Public* and *The Great Tradition* had endorsed.

The Preface argues that those critics whose account of Dickens's Art would deny him 'marked intellectual powers—a capacity, for example, to read and understand Bentham' are mistaken. And one of the useful strands of the Dickens book is Queenie Leavis's insistence that the reactions of the Victorians themselves (for example those of Dickens's friend and biographer John Forster) are often a better guide to the understanding of Dickens than the psychological jargon of modern biographers and critics. Yet surely the fact that there is no account of Dickens having studied Bentham in Forster is evidence against rather than for the Leavis case. Moreover the Benthamite *Saturday Review* critics (who included the Leavis's admired Leslie Stephen) were contemptuous of Dickens's understanding of social matters and of his sentimental philanthropy. However, it could be claimed, more tenuously, that Dickens had sensed the underlying spirit of Benthamism, and that the very contempt of these critics, in their Benthamite mood, evidences this. In any case *Dickens the Novelist* is a book which no responsible reader of Dickens can afford to ignore. It shows that Dickens was 'the great entertainer', yes, but that he combined this with an imaginative exploration of the problems of his age which would be comprehensible to his contemporaries without, at its best, sacrificing subtlety. Take the Meagles family in *Little Dorrit*: 'it is quite unjust to assume that Dickens "endorses" simple-mindedly Mr Meagles's sermon to Tattycoram', writes Queenie Leavis defending the novel against R. Garis's attack. Leavis makes a strong case for the view that 'the usual easy and confident denial of any profundity of thought to Dickens is absurd and shameful' in a subtle analysis of *Little Dorrit* in which the reality of Little Dorrit (as opposed to the

'contrived unreality' of Little Nell) is skilfully defended and
Queenie Leavis has a superb defence of the portrayal of Pip in
Great Expectations against *simpliste* charges of snobbery. Her
account of the nature of the relationship between Dickens
and Tolstoy in the essay on *David Copperfield* is interesting,
but the suggestion of an influence of portrayal of the David-
Dora relationship on that of the Prince Andrew–Lise
relationship is unconvincing.

VI. LEAVIS, LAWRENCE AND ELIOT

In many ways Leavis's engagement with Lawrence has done
harm to both. It has encouraged Leavis to over-indulge that
sectarian certainty of righteousness which, tempered by his
other qualities of flexibility and perceptiveness, gives an
exhilarating astringency to his work, but which, left to
luxuriate alone, too much encouraged Leavis to allow mere
assertion to replace analysis of the type discussed earlier in
this survey. At the same time it has allowed those who dislike
Lawrence to find support for their dislike in the sometimes
injudicious tone of his admirer. The admiration was not
always injudicious. The essay on Lawrence written in the
same year as Lawrence's death (1930) and printed in *For
Continuity* is a most creditable piece of work about a recent
author, despite Leavis's later reservations about it. Lawrence's
preoccupation with the primitive is criticized as fostering 'in
him a certain inhumanity' and *The Rainbow* and *Women in
Love* are singled out as remarkable, but, nevertheless, flawed
works which buy 'a strange intensity' at the price of a limited
range. At this stage Lawrence's discursive works, such as
Fantasia of the Unconscious were only to be considered at all
because of Lawrence's artistic achievements in his other
works, a far cry from the way they are wholeheartedly
endorsed in *Thought, Words and Creativity*. But in the essay
'D. H. Lawrence and Professor Irving Babbitt' written in
1932 and also included in *For Continuity* a new note is already
heard. We are at the beginning of that use of Lawrence as a
touchstone for bringing out the deficiencies of Eliot, and, in

particular, the failure of Eliot's periodical *The Criterion* for which Lawrence has been 'an opportunity and a test'. The theme of Eliot's deficiencies is to become a more and more insistent one in Leavis's later books. When Leavis with his wife and other collaborators embarked on the production of their own journal *Scrutiny*, the most important critical periodical of the twentieth century, the fate of *The Criterion* stood as an awful warning to them.

The first number of *Scrutiny* appeared in May 1932 and the journal ran as a quarterly until October 1953. Two substantial anthologies of it were made: Eric Bentley's *The Importance of Scrutiny* published in 1948, reprinted 1964, and Leavis's own *A Selection from Scrutiny* in two volumes published by Cambridge University Press in 1968. None of the contributors or editors was paid and the periodical worked only because of their devotion, that of the editorial board (from 1934 Leavis, L. C. Knights, Denys Thompson and D. W. Harding), and particularly of Queenie Leavis and Leavis himself. Because of demand the set was reprinted by C.U.P. in 1963. As I have said *The Calendar of Modern Letters* was a significant inspiration for the enterprise. Little in the way of poetry or fiction was included but, as was consonant with Leavis's concern to link literature with other concerns, the range of subjects covered was much wider than literature proper. Articles on philosophy, politics, education, sociology and psychology were published. James Smith, Martin Turnell and Dennis Enright contributed work on Italian, French and German culture. D. W. Harding, one of the most distinguished contributors, was later to become Professor of Psychology at the University of London. Much of Leavis's own published work originally appeared in the periodical. At first *Scrutiny* was quite abreast of the contemporary scene, but some have felt, perhaps justly, that earlier figures like Joyce, Yeats, Mann and Proust were never adequately encompassed, and that in the 1940s the immediately contemporary began to be too dismissively dealt with. Yet even here it might be claimed that this course was far better than the attempt to 'keep up' which so often leads to a shallow facility. An editor, like a critic, must be allowed his economies.

There is, unfortunately, a not unwarranted suspicion that Leavis's growing exaltation of Lawrence at Eliot's expense was not entirely disinterested, for we now know that Eliot, on the strength of his admiration for Leavis's pamphlet *Mass Civilization and Minority Culture*, had commissioned a piece for *The Criterion* which he had then decided not to use—a most delicate situation. Ronald Hayman says that the substance of the piece appeared in *Scrutiny* for September 1932 under the title 'What's Wrong with Criticism?' It is not unreasonable to suppose that Leavis's rejection by the poet whose innovative work he had so strongly championed must have cut deeply. As late as 1976 in the Spring issue of *New Universities Quarterly* a rankling resentment against the poet can be detected underlying Leavis's strange account of a visit by Eliot to see him in Cambridge in 1940 or 1941. Leavis prefaces it by saying that 'Although we rarely met and rarely corresponded, Eliot and I knew each other well. The knowledge was a matter of finding each other so very uncongenial as to generate a great deal of awareness—on my side, certainly diagnostic.' Leavis ends by making the extraordinary claim that he (Leavis) was 'a major focus of the guilt feelings expressed in *The Family Reunion*, the most revealingly personal of his works'.

I have suggested that it might be the case that some of Leavis's hostility towards Milton is directed not so much against Milton (its ostensible object) as against some of Milton's classically-trained apologists. The view that Leavis's criticism of Lawrence is, both in its praise of Lawrence and in some of its attacks on Lawrence's critics, not disinterested in the same way that the criticism of Swift or Pope in *The Common Pursuit* is disinterested, can I think be advanced with even more confidence. *D. H. Lawrence: Novelist* (1955), for all its undoubted usefulness to the sympathetic reader of Lawrence (to the unsympathetic reader it will only act as a further irritant) marks the beginning of a decline in Leavis's work as a strictly literary critic (his real *forte*), a decline only partially redeemed by his interesting essay on *Anna Karenina* and his long analysis of Eliot's *Four Quartets* in *The Living Principle*. Leavis occasionally makes concessions about weaknesses in Lawrence, or speaks of the special difficulties

Lawrence had, but these concessions and qualifications have curiously little effect on a too continuous acclamation (sometimes insufficiently supported by analysis) of Lawrence's consummate artistry, moral insight and lack of defects as both man and writer. The claim that Lawrence's best works are 'dramatic poems' sometimes seems part of a bid to capture assent, by means of persuasive nomenclature, to the view that the novel can be approached as poetry. Leavis oscillates between the view that Lawrence's works are continuous with those of George Eliot and Tolstoy and should have nothing in them that would disconcert admirers of those two novelists, and the view that he undertook radical departures from their vision, scope and mode of presentation. I feel an uneasy strain between the simultaneous acclamation of Lawrence's creative–exploratory quality and his quality of convincingness and verisimilitude as when Hermione in *Women in Love* is praised as 'triumphantly a character', and the dialogue in that book is called 'convincingly dramatic in every respect'. The difficulties raised by Lawrence's intriguing mixture of realism and symbolism (for all Leavis's repudiation of the latter term he has to use it) are never really faced. For example is Gerald Crich's father sufficiently convincing as an actual mine owner (in the way Hermione is convincing as a society hostess) to carry Lawrence's poignant indictment of industrial society, an indictment Gerald himself is also somewhat unconvincingly used to sustain? But perhaps the most baffling part of *D. H. Lawrence: Novelist* is the sixth chapter, which presents what Michael Tanner has justly called a 'grotesquely high' estimate of 'St. Mawr'. Leavis claims that 'St. Mawr' presents 'a creative and technical originality more remarkable' than that of Eliot's *The Waste Land*. This part of the book in particular is more remarkable for assertion and will (oddly enough characteristics against which both Leavis and Lawrence protest) than for analysis. Once again one feels that hostility to Eliot and to the Bloomsbury with which Leavis now associates him, is the real motive behind many of the remarks and not a disinterested critical engagement with Lawrence's text.

In the appendix to *D. H. Lawrence: Novelist*, Leavis called the twentieth century in English literature 'the age of D. H.

Lawrence and T. S. Eliot', and, if we thought the balance in Leavis's work had swung too much to a preoccupation with Lawrence, Leavis certainly redressed this with his account of *Four Quartets* in *The Living Principle* (1975), an account which Christopher Ricks rightly called 'the most sustained piece of criticism that he has ever produced, of a single work of poetry or of prose'. It is impossible to deal in a short compass with these deeply engaged prose reflections on poems, which, if uneven, contain passages that constitute some of the finest poetic meditation of the twentieth century. Both Eliot's poetry and Leavis's reflections on it call for constant frequentation. Perhaps the main point I can make about Leavis's reflections on it here is to say that they are criticism in which Leavis for the first time unequivocally operates with a discursive criterion, by which I mean a criterion which is applied to the contents of a poem irrespective of their formal embodiment. Whereas previously Leavis had been concerned with ideas only in so far as they were poetically realized, he now questions Eliot's ideas in themselves, independently of any poetic realization of them. This is perhaps particularly evident when Leavis claims that there can be no really coherent presentation of a transcendent reality and that 'time is an essential constituent of reality' and cannot truly be said to be unreal in the way that the 'Bradleyan' Eliot asserts it to be. Leavis's critique is salutary and important as showing that, contrary to Mallarmé's often quoted and pernicious dictum, poetry *is* made with ideas as well as with words and that this is the case even with a so apparently 'musical' and 'non-discursive' work as *Four Quartets*. The depth of the outrage Eliot's ideas offer to Leavis's own beliefs, the sense Leavis has that his answers to the questions Eliot poses 'are not Eliot's' are what have provoked Leavis's clear dissent from the discursive and paraphrasable 'wisdom' Eliot's lines offer, indeed the seeing of much of it as unwisdom.

VALEDICTION

I had originally thought of ending this survey of Leavis's work with a portrayal of the Leavis of such later books as

English Literature in our Time and the University (1967) and
Nor Shall My Sword (1972) as, like D. H. Lawrence's Birkin
in *Women in Love*, a kind of would-be prophet or *salvator
mundi* figure, but one unredeemed, alas, by the dramatic
testing and ironic scrutiny through which Lawrence 'places'
Birkin, and one, moreover, subject to an illusory view of
institutions (such as the 'University', or, for that matter,
'English Literature') which his hero Lawrence would have
treated with irreverent insouciance and despatched to the
lumber room of outmoded ideals and belated postures. But
to end an account of the greatest literary critic of the twentieth
century on such a note would be ungracious, especially in the
shadow of his recent death. We shall have to contend with
many winds of doctrine blowing from the camps of various
embattled orthodoxies, and one or other of them, may,
perhaps, in the end, sweep us off our feet, but the critical work
of Leavis at his best is, despite what his enemies say, no such
orthodoxy among others, but a source of energy and strength
and insight enabling us to investigate the attitudes underlying
any orthodoxy (or heterodoxy) through a close engagement
with the style in which those attitudes present themselves.
Leavis's own energy of mind found an adequate and complex
vehicle in a supple and scrupulously self-qualifying style
which was for far too long subject to belle-lettristic detraction
If Leavis has 'troubled' some, then we may say with René
Char that '*Ce qui vient au monde pour ne rien troubler ne mérite
ni égards ni patience*'; 'Whoever comes into the world to
trouble nothing merits neither respect nor patience'. One
wants to retort to cavillings about praise of Leavis in the way
that E. M. Forster retorted to Eliot's cavillings about his
praise of Lawrence on Lawrence's death: 'There are occasions
when I would rather feel like a fly than a spider.'

There is a fine passage by Henrik Von Wright on a great
philosopher with whom Leavis himself had a somewhat
equivocal relationship, Wittgenstein. Indeed, Leavis's interesting 'Memories of Wittgenstein', published in *The Human
World* for February 1973 are not, perhaps, free of a certain
undercurrent of feeling that Wittgenstein was a kind of rival.
The 'Memories' certainly bring out incidentally how
intensely 'local', Cambridge, a man Leavis was as opposed to

the 'agoraphobic', almost 'displaced' philosopher. I should like to conclude by quoting this passage because it seems to me to apply just as strikingly to Leavis himself if we substitute his name in it for that of Wittgenstein:

To learn from Wittgenstein without coming to adopt his form of expression and catch-words and even to imitate his tone of voice, his mien and gestures, was almost impossible. The danger was that the thoughts should degenerate into a jargon. The teaching of great men often has a simplicity and naturalness which makes the difficult appear easy to grasp. Their disciples usually become, therefore, insignificant epigones. The historic significance of such men does not manifest itself in their disciples but through influences of a more indirect, subtle and, often, unexpected kind.

F. R. LEAVIS

A Select Bibliography

(Place of publication London, unless otherwise stated)

Bibliography:

F. R. LEAVIS. A CHECK LIST 1924–64 by D. F. Mackenzie and M.-P. Allum (1966).

Separate Works:

MASS CIVILIZATION AND MINORITY CULTURE (1930).

D. H. LAWRENCE (1930).

NEW BEARINGS IN ENGLISH POETRY (1932)
—contains 'Poetry and the Modern World', 'The Situation at the End of the War', 'T. S. Eliot', 'Ezra Pound', 'Gerard Manley Hopkins'.

HOW TO TEACH READING: A PRIMER FOR EZRA POUND (1932).

FOR CONTINUITY (1933)
—contains 'Marxism and Cultural Continuity', 'Mass Civilization and Minority Culture', 'The Literary Mind', 'What's Wrong with Criticisms', 'Babbitt buys the World', 'Arnold Bennett: American Version', 'John Dos Passos', 'D. H. Lawrence', 'D. H. Lawrence and Professor Irving Babbitt', 'Under Which King, Bezonian?', 'Restatements for Critics', 'This Poetical Renascence', 'Joyce and "The Revolution of the Word"'.

CULTURE AND ENVIRONMENT (with Denys Thompson) (1933).

TOWARDS STANDARDS OF CRITICISM: *Selections from the Calendar of Modern Letters, 1925–27.* Edited with an Introduction by F. R. Leavis (1933).

DETERMINATIONS: Edited with an Introduction by F. R. Leavis (1934)
—contains 'On Metaphysical Poetry' by J. Smith; 'Marvell's Garden' by W. Empson; 'A Note on Nostalgia' by D. W. Harding; 'The Irony of Swift' by F. R. Leavis; 'Notes on Comedy' by L. C. Knights; 'Burns' by J. Speirs; 'John Webster' by W. A. Edwards; '*XXX Cantos* of Ezra Pound' by R. Bottrall; 'Our Debt to Lamb' by D. Thompson; 'I. A. Richards' by D. W. Harding; 'The New Bentham' by M. Oakeshott; 'The Scientific Best-Seller' by J. L. Russell.

REVALUATION: TRADITION AND DEVELOPMENT IN ENGLISH POETRY (1936)
—contains 'The Line of Wit', 'Milton's Verse', 'Pope', 'The Augustan Tradition', 'Wordsworth', 'Shelley', 'Keats'.

EDUCATION AND THE UNIVERSITY: A SKETCH FOR AN ENGLISH SCHOOL (1943)

—contains 'The Idea of a University', 'A Sketch for an English School', 'Literary Studies', Appendix: 'T. S. Eliot's Later Poetry', 'How to teach Reading'.

THE GREAT TRADITION: GEORGE ELIOT, HENRY JAMES, JOSEPH CONRAD (1948)
—contains 'The Great Tradition', 'George Eliot', 'Henry James', 'Joseph Conrad', *Hard Times*: An Analytic Note', Appendix: '*Daniel Deronda*: A Conversation by Henry James'.

MILL ON BENTHAM AND COLERIDGE. With an Introduction (1950).

THE COMMON PURSUIT (1952)
—contains 'Mr Eliot and Milton', 'In Defence of Milton', 'Gerard Manley Hopkins', 'The Letters of Gerard Manley Hopkins', 'The Irony of Swift', '*The Dunciad*', 'Johnson and Augustanism', 'Johnson as Poet', 'Tragedy and the Medium', 'Diabolic Intellect and the Noble Hero', '*Measure for Measure*', 'The Criticism of Shakespeare's Late Plays', 'Literature and Society', 'Sociology and Literature', 'Bunyan Through Modern Eyes', 'Literary Criticism and Philosophy', 'The Wild Untutored Phoenix', 'Mr Eliot, Mr Wyndham Lewis and Lawrence', 'The Logic of Christian Discrimination', 'Keynes, Lawrence and Cambridge', 'E. M. Forster', 'Approaches to T. S. Eliot', 'The Progress of Poetry'.

THE COMPLEX FATE by Marius Bewley: Introduction and two Interpolations by Leavis (1952).

D. H. LAWRENCE, NOVELIST (1955)
—contains Introduction, 'Lawrence and Art: The Lesser Novels', 'Lawrence and Class: *The Daughters of the Vicar*', 'Lawrence and Tradition: *The Rainbow*', '*Women in Love*', '*The Captain's Doll*', '*St Mawr*', '*The Tales*', 'Note: *Being an Artist*', Appendix: 'Mr Eliot and Lawrence'.

TWO CULTURES? THE SIGNIFICANCE OF C. P. SNOW (1962)
—contains the 1962 Richmond Lecture with an essay by Michael Yudkin on C. P. Snow's 1959 Rede Lecture.

ANNA KARENINA AND OTHER ESSAYS (1967)
—contains '*Anna Karenina*', 'Johnson as Critic', '*The Pilgrim's Progress*', '*Adam Bede*', '*The Europeans*', '*What Maisie Knew*', '*The Shadow-Line*', '*The Secret Sharer*', '*Pudd'nhead Wilson*', 'The Americanness of American Literature', '*The Complex Fate*', 'Pound in his Letters', ' "Lawrence Scholarship" and Lawrence', 'T. S. Eliot as Critic', 'Towards Standards of Criticism', 'The Orthodoxy of Enlightenment'.

LECTURES IN AMERICA (with Q. D. Leavis) (1969)
—contains 'Luddites? or There is Only One Culture', 'Eliot's Classical Standing', 'Yeats: The Problem and the Challenge', by F. R. Leavis. 'A Fresh Approach to *Wuthering Heights*', by Q. D. Leavis.

ENGLISH LITERATURE IN OUR TIME AND THE UNIVERSITY, The Clark
Lectures (1969)

—contains 'Literature and the University: the wrong question',
'The Present and the Past: Eliot's demonstration', 'Eliot's "axe to
grind" and the nature of great criticism', 'Why *Four Quartets*
matters in a Technologico-Benthamite age', 'The Necessary
Opposite, Lawrence: Illustration—the opposed critics on *Hamlet*',
Summing-Up: ' "Monstrous unrealism" and the alternative',
Appendices: 'The Function of the University', 'Rilke on Vacuity',
'Research in English'.

DICKENS THE NOVELIST (with Q. D. Leavis) (1970)

—contains 'The First Major Novel: *Dombey and Son*', '*Hard Times:*
The World of Bentham', 'Dickens and Blake: *Little Dorrit*', by
F. R. Leavis, 'Dickens and Tolstoy: The case for a serious view of
David Copperfield', '*Bleak House:* A Chancery World', 'How we
must read *Great Expectations*', 'The Dickens Illustrations: Their
Function', by Q. D. Leavis.

NOR SHALL MY SWORD: DISCOURSES ON PLURALISM, COMPASSION AND
SOCIAL HOPE (1972)

—contains Introductory: 'Life is a Necessary Word', 'Two Cultures?
the significance of Lord Snow', 'Luddites? or There is Only One
Culture', ' "English", unrest and continuity', ' "Literarism versus
Scientism": The Misconception and the Menace', 'Pluralism,
Compassion and Social Hope', 'Elites, Oligarchies and an Educated
Public'.

LETTERS IN CRITICISM, edited with an Introduction by John Tasker
(1974)

—a collection of letters written by F. R. Leavis to newspapers and
periodicals between 1932 and 1973.

THE LIVING PRINCIPLE: 'ENGLISH' AS A DISCIPLINE OF THOUGHT (1975)

—contains 'Thought, Language and Objectivity', 'Judgment and
Analysis', 'Thought and Emotional Quality', 'Imagery and Move-
ment', 'Reality and Sincerity', 'Prose', '*Antony and Cleopatra* and
All for Love', '*Four Quartets*'.

THOUGHT, WORDS AND CREATIVITY (1976)

—contains analyses of D. H. Lawrence's *The Plumed Serpent, Women
in Love, The Captain's Doll* and *The Rainbow*.

Uncollected Essays and Reviews

'Dr Richards, Bentham and Coleridge', review of *Coleridge on
Imagination* by I. A. Richards in *Scrutiny* III, March 1935.

'Mr Auden's Talent', review of *Look Stranger* by W. H. Auden, *The*

Ascent of F6 by W. H. Auden and Christopher Isherwood in *Scrutiny* V, December 1936.

'Revaluations (XI): Arnold as Critic' in *Scrutiny* VII, December 1938.

'Hart Crane from this Side', review of *The Collected Poems of Hart Crane* in *Scrutiny* VII, March 1939.

'Revaluations (XIII): Coleridge in Criticism' in *Scrutiny* IX, June 1940; 'Hardy the Poet' in *Southern Review* vi, 1940–41.

'James as Critic', Introduction to *Henry James: Selected Literary Criticism*, ed. Morris Shapira. Heinemann, London.

'Justifying One's Valuation of Balke', Lecture at Bristol University. Printed in *The Human World*, No. 7, May 1972.

'Memories of Wittgenstein' in *The Human World*, No. 10, February 1973.

' "Believing in" the University' in *The Human World*, Nos. 15–16, May–August 1974.

'Mutually Necessary' in *New Universities Quarterly*, March 1976.

Biographical and Critical Studies

'Poetic v. Rhetorical Exegesis: the case for Leavis against Richards and Empson', by Mr McLuhan, *Sewanee* Review (April 1933).

A GATHERING OF FUGITIVES, by L. Trilling (1957)
—contains 'Dr Leavis and the Moral Tradition'.

'Mr Leavis on Literary Studies', by W. W. Robson, *Universities Quarterly XI* (February 1957).

'F. R. Leavis's *How to Teach Reading*', by D. Davie, *Essays in Criticism*, (July 1957).

POETRY AND MORALITY: STUDIES ON THE CRITICISM OF MATTHEW ARNOLD, T. S. ELIOT, F. R. LEAVIS, by V. Buckley (1959).

CULTURE AND SOCIETY, 1780–1950, by R. Williams (1959).

'Our Debt to Dr Leavis—A Symposium', by R. Williams, R. J. Kaufmann and A. Jones, *Critical Quarterly* (Autumn 1959).

THE LIVING MILTON, ed. F. Kermode (1960)
—contains 'Criticism and the Milton controversy', by B. Bergonzi.

THE CHARTED MIRROR: LITERARY AND CRITICAL ESSAYS, by J. Holloway (1960)
—contains 'The "New Establishment" in Criticism'.

'Men and Ideas: F. R. Leavis', by George Steiner, *Encounter* (May 1962)—reprinted in *Language and Silence* (1967) and *20th Century Literary Criticism*, ed. D. Lodge (1972).

F. R. LEAVIS: SOME ASPECTS OF HIS WORK, ed. C. D. Narasimhaiah, Mysore (1963).

MILTON'S GRAND STYLE by C. Ricks (1963).

LITERARY VIEWS: CRITICAL AND HISTORICAL, ed. C. Camden, Chicago (1964)
—contains 'The Literary Criticism of F. R. Leavis', by R. Wellek.

'The Use of "Concreteness" as an Evaluative Term in F. R. Leavis's *The Great Tradition*', by John Killham, *British Journal of Aesthetics*, January 1965.

CRITICAL ESSAYS, by W. W. Robson (1966)
—contains 'Mr Leavis on Literary Studies'.

THE LANGUAGE OF CRITICISM, by J. Casey (1966).

'Scrutiny's Failure with Shakespeare' by J. M. Newton, *Cambridge Quarterly*, Vol. I, No. 2 (Spring 1966).

THE RISE AND FALL OF THE MAN OF LETTERS, by J. Gross (1969).

THE SURVIVAL OF ENGLISH: ESSAYS IN CRITICISM OF LANGUAGE, by I. Robinson (1972).

THE METROPOLITAN CRITIC, by C. James (1974).

'Leavis at 80—what has his influence been?' A Symposium edited by P. French with contributions from D. W. Harding, L. C. Knights, M. C. Bradbrook and others, *The Listener* (24 July 1975).

'F. R. Leavis; b. 1895: Stability and Growth'. Contributions by M. Tanner, A. Gomme, M. Black, F. Inclis, D. Holbrook and others, *Universities Quarterly XXX*, 1 (Winter 1975).

LEAVIS, by R. Hayman (1976).

'But Yes' (a review of F. R. Leavis's *The Living Principle*), by C. Ricks, *Essays in Criticism*, October 1976.

'The Scrutiny Phenomenon', by F. W. Bateson, *The Sewanee Review*, Vol 85, 1977, pp. 144 152.

THE POET IN THE IMAGINARY MUSEUM, by Donald Davie (1977)
—contains an article prompted by Leavis's *Anna Karenina and Other Essays* (1967).

F. R. Leavis was closely associated with the foundation of *Scrutiny* in 1932 and joined the Editorial Board towards the end of that year. The journal was published continuously throughout the war and the final issue, the 76th with a Valedictory by Leavis appeared in October 1953. A photographic reprint of the complete set with an Index and a Retrospect by Leavis was published by the Cambridge University Press in 1963. Eric Bentley edited a volume of selections from *Scrutiny* entitled *The Importance of Scrutiny* which was published in the US in 1948 and reprinted in paperback in 1964 and F. R. Leavis himself brought out a paperback two-volume *Selection for Scrutiny* with CUP in 1968.

WRITERS AND THEIR WORK

SHERIDAN: W. A. Darlington
SMART: Geoffrey Grigson
SMOLLETT: Laurence Brander
STEELE, ADDISON: A. R. Humphreys
STERNE: D. W. Jefferson
SWIFT: J. Middleton Murry (1955)
SWIFT: A. Norman Jeffares (1976)
VANBRUGH: Bernard Harris
HORACE WALPOLE: Hugh Honour

Nineteenth Century:
ARNOLD: Kenneth Allott
AUSTEN: S. Townsend Warner (1951)
AUSTEN: B. C. Southam (1975)
BAGEHOT: N. St John-Stevas
THE BRONTË SISTERS:
         Phyllis Bentley (1950)
THE BRONTËS: I & II: Winifred Gérin
E. B. BROWNING: Alethea Hayter
ROBERT BROWNING: John Bryson
SAMUEL BUTLER: G. D. H. Cole
BYRON: I, II & III: Bernard Blackstone
CARLYLE: David Gascoyne (1952)
CARLYLE: Ian Campbell (1978)
CARROLL: Derek Hudson
CLOUGH: Isobel Armstrong
COLERIDGE: Kathleen Raine
CREEVEY & GREVILLE: J. Richardson
DE QUINCEY: Hugh Sykes Davies
DICKENS: K. J. Fielding
   EARLY NOVELS: T. Blount
   LATER NOVELS: B. Hardy
DISRAELI: Paul Bloomfield
GEORGE ELIOT: Lettice Cooper
FITZGERALD: Joanna Richardson
GASKELL: Miriam Allott
GISSING: A. C. Ward
HARDY: R. A. Scott-James
          and C. Day Lewis
HAZLITT: J. B. Priestley (1960)
HAZLITT: R. L. Brett (1977)
HOOD: Laurence Brander
HOPKINS: Geoffrey Grigson
T. H. HUXLEY: William Irvine
KEATS: Edmund Blunden (1950)
KEATS: Miriam Allott (1976)
LAMB: Edmund Blunden
LANDOR: G. Rostrevor Hamilton

LEAR: Joanna Richardson
MACAULAY: G. R. Potter (1959)
MACAULAY: Kenneth Young (1976)
MEREDITH: Phyllis Bartlett
MILL: Maurice Cranston
MORRIS: P. Henderson
NEWMAN: J. M. Cameron
PATER: Ian Fletcher
PEACOCK: J. I. M. Stewart
CHRISTINA ROSSETTI: G. Battiscombe
D. G. ROSSETTI: Oswald Doughty
RUSKIN: Peter Quennell
SCOTT: Ian Jack
SHELLEY: G. M. Matthews
SOUTHEY: Geoffrey Carnall
STEPHEN: Phyllis Grosskurth
STEVENSON: G. B. Stern
SWINBURNE: Ian Fletcher
TENNYSON: B. C. Southam
THACKERAY: Laurence Brander
FRANCIS THOMPSON: P. Butter
TROLLOPE: Hugh Sykes Davies
WILDE: James Laver
WORDSWORTH: Helen Darbishire

Twentieth Century:
ACHEBE: A. Ravenscroft
ARDEN: Glenda Leeming
AUDEN: Richard Hoggart
BECKETT: J-J. Mayoux
BELLOC: Renée Haynes
BENNETT: Frank Swinnerton (1950)
BENNETT: Kenneth Young (1975)
BETJEMAN: John Press
BLUNDEN: Alec M. Hardie
BOND: Simon Trussler
BRIDGES: J. Sparrow
BURGESS: Carol M. Dix
CAMPBELL: David Wright
CARY: Walter Allen
CHESTERTON: C. Hollis
CHURCHILL: John Connell
COLLINGWOOD: E. W. F. Tomlin
COMPTON-BURNETT: R. Glynn Grylls
CONRAD: Oliver Warner (1950)
CONRAD: C. B. Cox (1977)
DE LA MARE: Kenneth Hopkins
NORMAN DOUGLAS: Ian Greenlees